SPIRITS
OF RANCHO
BUENA VISTA
ADOBE

SPIRITS
OF RANCHO
BUENA VISTA
ADOBE

NICOLE STRICKLAND

WITH CONTRIBUTIONS FROM ALI SCHREIBER

Haunted
America

Published by Haunted America
A Division of The History Press
Charleston, SC
www.historypress.com

Cover photo courtesy of Nicole Strickland.

First published 2018

Manufactured in the United States

ISBN 9781467139472

Library of Congress Control Number: 2018942431

For Gabe and Juan—your memories eternally reign in the heart and soul of the universe.

CONTENTS

FOREWORD

Southern California, popularly known today as "So Cal," is synonymous with wealth, glamour and entertainment. Millennia ago, Native American tribes searched for food and water in a great undeveloped expanse of desert leading to the Pacific Ocean. Many of those tribes no longer exist, and with good reason. Spanish explorers, along with neighboring Mexicans, appeared and claimed the land, leaving their mark by establishing forts, missions and small towns, which were privately held. What happened to those structures and places is laid out precisely in the sequence of events from the earliest migrants to the gold miners in Northern California who looked to the south for their food and supplies.

The history revealed in this book is as much about the land as it is about the people who lived there. Missions, rancho lands with thousands of grazing cattle and squalid adobe homes with dirt floors made for a hardscrabble life. But the never-ending feuds over the land itself as it was claimed, reclaimed and bitterly contested make for a most interesting read. Vast tracts became smaller and smaller until commercialization finally took over in the last century. A few notable exceptions escaped destruction, one of them being the Rancho Buena Vista Adobe.

Into this saga of early California history, explored and retold with methodical precision and yet with a liveliness matching the fervor of the times and the souls who fashioned elegance from the impoverished mud, enters author Nicole Strickland. Long credited with impeccable credentials as a paranormal researcher and gifted with an engaging writing style that breathes vibrant new life into the dead facts of history, Strickland is quite at home with ghosts as the active (and often distinctly noisy!) artifacts of humanity's irrepressible urge to live, express and survive.

There is plenty of hard work reflected in these pages and unmistakably a labor of love as well in the patient uncovering of the ownership history and the accounts of the quixotic people who lived there, with the imposing land itself being both a cherished prize and a rugged adversary. The spirits of people who were born there, maintained and improved the property and often died there seem to still be alert and waiting to tell their stories. In years of studying this adobe landmark, Nicole Strickland and her paranormal research team have documented many noteworthy eerie occurrences that cannot be easily explained, much less dismissed.

In the chapters that follow, you are simultaneously confronted by the grim, relentless march of history with a wealth of detail born of dreams and dust but also warmly welcomed with gregarious hospitality to help restore the destinies of lingering spirits that persist in their old habitations, hovering in a net of nostalgia between familiar desert comforts and the lure of heaven's gate.

Gary Mantz and Suzanne Mitchell
Co-hosts, *Mantz and Mitchell*
1150 KKNW Seattle

ACKNOWLEDGEMENTS

It is always an honor to write a book about a renowned historical location. Writing is a way of life and completely soothes the soul. It is a proud moment to have finished this manuscript, as it's been many years in the making. There are many people who have helped this book transition from thought to reality, and it wouldn't have come into existence without their tireless assistance and contributions.

First and foremost, I want to give thanks to my mom, Norma Strickland, and my dad, Byron Strickland, for their eternal support and love. It's a great feeling to know that your parents are proud of the work you've done. I love you both so much.

Sincere gratitude extends to Ali Schreiber, my soul sister, San Diego Paranormal Research Society co-director and comrade in arms. I am so appreciative of you and all your assistance and many invaluable contributions to this book. You and I have such a beautifully intertwined work ethic and approach to interacting with spirits; perhaps, many of the experiences we've encountered at the Rancho Buena Vista Adobe wouldn't have even occurred without the presence of both of us. Our work and friendship will continue on for eternity.

I offer my heartfelt thanks to the Arcadia Publishing/History Press staff for believing in my work. Thank you to Laurie Krill, my acquisitions editor, for her tireless dedication to my book, seeing it in its early stages all the way to completion.

ACKNOWLEDGEMENTS

Thank you to Gary Mantz and Suzanne Mitchell for writing this book's foreword. Mantz and Mitchell are the co-hosts of the popular *Mantz and Mitchell* terrestrial radio show, which airs live in Seattle, Washington, on KKNW 1150 AM on Fridays from 10:00 a.m. to 11:00 a.m. and Saturdays from 10:00 a.m. to 12:00 p.m.

The City of Vista has been an ongoing supporter for our monthly Spirits of the Adobe tours. Much gratitude extends to the City of Vista management team, employees Bill Fortmueller, Rob Anderson and Kim Crawford for assistance in co-creating these fundraising tours as well as helping us to co-manage them. Additionally, we are extremely grateful to the City of Vista and the Friends of the Rancho Buena Vista Adobe for their tireless preservation and upkeep of the legendary rancho. Much thanks to employees Fred Tracy and Frank Rojano for providing their unique paranormal encounters. Thank you for all that you do.

Much appreciation to Stephanie Arias and Samuel Wylie at the Huntington Library for helping us with historical Cave Johnson Couts journals and Rancho Buena Vista Adobe history. Thank you for all your help in arranging for Ali Schreiber and me to visit the library archives.

Ali and I also extend our gratitude to all of our Spirits of the Adobe tour guests for supporting the tours' fundraising efforts for the Friends of the Rancho Buena Vista Adobe. The majority of the discussed supernatural encounters in this book occurred during the tours. We thank each and every one of you for your attendance and interaction with the spirits of the adobe. It means so much to the ongoing preservation of the rancho's legacy.

Last but certainly not least, I extend our sincere thanks and gratitude to the many spirits that continue to call the Rancho Buena Vista Adobe home. You are honored, revered and loved. Both Ali and I thank you so much for allowing us to enter your world and learn about your stories. It's been a profound privilege to build a rapport with all of the spirits of the adobe, many being past residents of the property during its heyday. Today, along with historical preservation, their existence continues to educate guests on the noted site's chronological tapestry. We look forward to future research projects and tours where we can continue our quest in communicating with the spirits of the adobe.

INTRODUCTION

Vista is older than 100 years. Much older. People have been going through here—through this particular spot—for ages. In fact, it was "Buena Vista" 60 years before 1882. First came the Aborigines—the Indians. Then came the Explorers, followed by the Mission Padres and the Pathfinders of 200 years ago. Today, at the junction of Vista Way and Santa Fe, we are standing on the very ground over which they trod or rode. For this is the original El Camino Real—the King's Highway!
—Harrison Doyle, Vista's noted historian

There's an interesting story that explains how Vista received its official name. When area settler John Frazier resided in the area, he boasted a mineral well and called his village "Frazier's Crossing." Frazier applied to the United States Post Office Department for a permit under this newly acquired namesake on September 1, 1882. He received notification saying that a Frazier Post Office already existed in Tulare County, so he was then advised to submit another name. He complied and presented the moniker "Vista." This second time around, the Post Office Department accepted the name, ultimately granting permission to open Vista's premiere post office on October 9, 1882.

In order to truly study the history of Vista, California, one must go back thousands of years to a vast land complete with rolling hills, indigenous plants and trees, Native American tribes and a splendid view of the Pacific Ocean. In fact, many native peoples inhabited this region of California during its early days. Some of the tribes are known, whereas others remain

A westward view from the Rancho Buena Vista Adobe depicts the vastly uninhabited terrain of Vista as photographed in 1885. *Courtesy of Vista Historical Society.*

elusive; however, one fact remains clear: Indians, in substantial numbers, have resided in all areas of the southwestern United States for thousands of years, especially in Southern California. The industrialized portions of Vista today exist in the same sites that the Indians gathered in, so there's always a reminder of the aborigines from hundreds of years ago.

The *Luiseños* and *Diegueños*, having arrived in Vista in later periods, are more commonly associated with the area. These individuals infiltrated Southern California coastal regions, extending from the southern portion of Los Angeles down to the northern portion of San Diego. The *Luiseños* constructed their villages along the San Luis Rey River and freely resided in Rancherias, which consisted of around one hundred people up until the founding of the San Luis Rey Mission in 1798. With the advent of the mission system, the land's indigenous peoples were coerced into the mission lifestyle adopted by the Spanish peoples. The mission era weakened by the 1830s with Mexico's independence from Spain.

The rancho period commenced when the Mexican government started to grant land ownerships to several individuals. During the time when California was governed by kings, royal army soldiers received Spain's premiere grants, as these servicemen differentiated themselves in service to their ruler as well as having joined the explorers and missionaries on their intrepid excursion to California. These individuals were the embodiment of courage, undergoing pioneering destitution while assisting in construction of the missions, pueblos and presidios.

During this time of vast expanses of land and cattle-covered grounds, approaches to land surveying and boundary establishments were significantly careless and negligent. In fact, the phrase "a little more or less" was exploited as a way to conceal mistakes in estimates. The surveyors commenced the process on horseback at a point designated by a tiny pile of stones or a tree or rock with an eccentric shape. R.W. Brackett's book *The History of San Diego County Ranchos* further asserts that land examination entailed "using a 50-foot length riata, tracts of land were measured; the inspection of one rancho was portrayed as starting from a hill upon which Don --- sits upon his white horse." With the exception of memoranda, there was very little record of these land endowments during the first half of Mexican predominance.

Rancho titling was quite a creative process. You see, the *ranchero* typically named his territory allowance after the patron saint of his family or the saint upon whose hallowed day the grant was established. Occasionally, an Indian name was utilized in naming his holdings, as was the case with Cave Johnson Couts's Rancho Guajome, or "Home of the Frogs." As is the case with "Buena Vista," i.e., "good view," regional description was employed in the official naming process.

After fifty years of Spanish predominance, in 1821, the Mexican government took over the land previously run by the missions and presidios. These territories were handed over to individuals who resided in the area as a way to promote agriculture and praise servicemen's loyal military service. Some of the most fertile land existed on the ranchos, generating grain, vegetables, fruits and other provisions. Additionally, thousands of cattle, sheep and horses grazed the hillsides. The *dons* and *donas*, also known as *rancheros*, owned these land tracts and constructed huge adobe ranch homes. Native Americans were also called upon to work in the houses, making up an entire workforce needed to run the rancho. Dancing, fiestas, rodeos and munificent hospitality pervaded the daily life at these homesteads.

Economic livelihood came in the form of land and cattle and the exporting of hides and tallow. In fact, by the 1820s, cattle were reared specifically for their hides and tallow, with around forty thousand sold abroad in one year. The Mexican government opened both the Monterey and San Diego ports to foreign traders by 1822. Between 1826 and 1848, English and Boston vessels transported around six million hides and seven thousand tons of tallow, with rancheros trading them for china, jewelry, linens, perfumes and other goods. For more than forty years, the Californio rancho way of life dominated, and Americans relocated to California in increasing numbers to seek new fortune and success. These individuals were so attracted to the area's new prospects that they became Catholic or Mexican citizens if their backgrounds or religions interfered with the right to hold territory. During Mexican rule, the number of private land grants skyrocketed from twenty to eight hundred.

The two remaining ranchos of Vista are the Rancho Buena Vista Adobe and the Rancho Guajome. They both are reminders of the adobe lifestyle during a time when the *dons* and *donas* reigned supreme. More than 150 years old, these adobe homes have been preserved and restored and today offer educational and historical programs for those wanting to saturate themselves in the rancho era of California. Just as Old Town is the historic gem of San Diego and the RMS *Queen Mary* is to Long Beach, these celebrated structures are the shining diamonds of Vista.

Vista was a quiet little village prior to 1912, when the Vista Land Company came into being. Further development of the region occurred in 1890 with the completion of the Oceanside-Escondido branch of the Santa Fe Railroad. A store and the aforementioned post office were erected in the present city of Vista. The affluent business, coordinated by Hartley-Martine Real Estate Company of Redlands, purchased a sizeable piece of the Rancho Buena Vista land. The corporation was credited with laying out roadways and constructing the Vista Inn. Old Highway 395 extended through Vista back then, and it took approximately two days to travel from San Diego to the Riverside area. With beautiful rolling hillsides, attractive climate and fruitful soil, land developers realized the potential of this sleepy little village during the 1920s.

The Vista Water Company, formed in 1911, helped to override the scarce water sources, as the area lacked a substantial source of irrigation water. The area became known as the avocado capital of the world when water was brought in from Lake Henshaw and a land zone of 2,100 acres was attained by an association led by Edwin G. Hart. This also helped with developing crops and citrus groves, one of the premier economic mainstays of Vista since the early days. The territory was subdivided into town lots and small farms, which promptly sold and signaled the swift development of the main town and neighboring area.

Vista's original settlers were a capable bunch, possessing knowledge in a variety of fields, including horticulture, land sales, construction and publishing. Within time, the sparsely occupied Vista started seeing the construction of residences along newly established dirt roads, as well as other enterprises. With the advent of the *Vista Press* in 1926, residents could advertise new business opportunities to the budding town. Indeed, the early residents of the promising town paved the way for its future populace, with many family generations choosing to stay in the area year after year. In the early 1960s, Vista chose to incorporate, and on January 28, 1963, it became known as the city of Vista.

When you drive through the city of Vista in modern times, you will run across little remnants of its past, which further enable you to appreciate its times gone by. By visiting the Rancho Guajome and/or the Rancho Buena Vista Adobe, you not only get a nostalgic glimpse of what life was like for early settlers but will also come to appreciate the work they put into their community. Situated in the northern region of San Diego County, the current Vista is a thriving community and family locale. There are numerous parks and recreational opportunities for the young and old. As

A front view of the Rancho Buena Vista Adobe across the street from Vista High School, circa 1930s or early 1940s. *Courtesy of Vista Historical Society.*

The Rancho Buena Vista Adobe's iconic courtyard fountain pictured in the late 1980s or early 1990s. *Courtesy of Vista Historical Society.*

the city changes over time, its residents continue to respect and revere the courageous people of its past.

For over seven years, it has been a pure pleasure to fundraise for the Friends of the Rancho Buena Vista Adobe by hosting monthly Spirits of the Adobe tours at the historic site. These tours not only tell the historical tales of the adobe's many owners but also give tourgoers an opportunity to communicate and interact with its many spiritual residents. Yes, this legendary landmark is known as one of the most haunted areas in all of Vista, and its ethereal residents continue to convey their stories in modern times. The rancho period was steeped in romance and pride, and perhaps its ghostly inhabitants choose to stay in the home they fell in love with many years ago. Their memories live on in the present through every single interaction with living guests who come to honor the heyday of the Rancho Buena Vista. The main premise of this book is to interweave the historical narrative along with the paranormal happenings of this beautiful rancho where echoes of the past continue to pulsate in the present. In doing so, we honor and commemorate the adobe and its past residents for serving the Vista community since the dawning of its days.

CHAPTER 1

The Historical Tapestry of the Rancho Buena Vista Adobe

The ranchos take us back to the colorful epochs of the Spanish and Mexican periods. They are inseparably a part of the state's romantic history, for there is hardly a grain field or orchard that is not traced directly to an old Spanish land grant.
—*Myrtle Garrison*, Romance and History of California Ranchos

Two hundred years ago, Native Americans roamed the land in search of food, water and other life-sustaining ingredients. The site of an ancient Indian village, Vista's native peoples originated from the Luiseños and Diegueños tribes. Gaspar de Portola and a group of Spaniards landed in the area in 1769, with both missionaries and Indians joining Mission San Luis Rey. The mission's premise was to encourage Christianity as well as self-sufficiency to aborigines. This also included developed knowledge of farming and the rearing of animals. Once this objective was met, the intent was to return the terrain to the Indians.

Vista occupies a unique spot in the topography of Southern California and the United States, with the Pacific Ocean to the west and Mexico and the city of San Diego to the south. Most historians concur that the earliest peoples to inhabit this region were Asians who traveled in immigrations from Siberia to Alaska some twenty thousand years ago. A second group of incomers arrived around 8,000 BC. These San Dieguitos were nomadic hunters and gatherers hailing from the Rocky Mountains and Sierra Nevada. Then, around 3,000 BC, the ancestors from San Diego's modern-day tribes migrated to the region. In the northern counties, such as Vista, the native aborigines belonged to the Uto-Aztecan family, with its Takic subfamily arriving to Southern California approximately one thousand years ago. This particular faction included the Luiseño, Cupeño and Cahuilla peoples.

The documentation of Native American residents in Southern California occurred when Spanish explorers visited the area in the 1500s. Voyagers Juan Cabrillo and Sebastian Vizcaino, among others, found these native peoples to be amicable and cooperative. The state's twenty-one missions were founded between 1769 and 1823, directly providing economic possibilities for the region. In 1769, the mission/presidio in San Diego was the premiere Spanish colony created in California. During this time, the Spanish and Mexican governments established missions, presidios and pueblos, thus commencing the period when substantial portions of rancho lands were handed over to private citizens.

Neophytes (Indians) were called upon to help with various trades, such as agriculture and carpentry, to help sustain the life of the mission system. The majority of the region's natives were attractive, healthy and happy peoples who intricately understood hunting and food-gathering techniques. They learned new skills and possessed knowledge of the Spanish language. Many of these natives worked on rancho lands and/or in towns after the disbanding of the California mission lifestyle. Sadly, the majority of Indian tribes affected by the California mission era are today extinct, as these natives' lives were radically affected when they were coerced into living at and working for these missions. One of the main reasons for this is evident in the Indians' lack of immunity to diseases brought by the influx of white men migrating to the San Diego region.

Historic Ranchos of San Diego by James S. Copley discusses how California's rancho period was intertwined with romanticism and further classified as the time between the dissolution of the Franciscan mission system and the state becoming Americanized, which commenced after the Mexican-American War. With the secularization of land in 1833, the rancho system controlled life in the Golden State up until 1846. With the commencing of the secularization of the California mission system in 1834, expansive territories of land were open to American traders, adventurists, soldiers and settlers. Native American conflicts ensued as the Mexican government separated San Diego's mission and the Mission San Luis Rey from religious connection in 1834. Undoubtedly, this paved the way for a tedious discord between the natives and Californios. During this time, feuds occurred between the men

A painted map depicting the "Ranchos of San Diego County" on one of the exterior walls of the gift shop. *Courtesy of Ali Schreiber.*

who were vowing for land; those who owned ranchos were considered kings during an epoch when the government lacked restrictions. Known as the Days of the Dons, this era was made up of two stages spanning the length of thirty years or so.

Shortly after the completion of secularization in 1840, both San Diego and the Mission San Luis Rey quarters witnessed the establishments of eighteen ranchos developed on previous mission lands or territories obtained by the missions. During the Mexican era, from 1821 to 1846, titles to land plots were contracted to individuals. The 1824 Mexican Colony Law instituted guidelines for the petitioning of California land grants; these rules were then stipulated in the Mexican Regulation (Reglamento). These decrees required the breakup of mission land domination and made it easier to obtain these territories. The primary intent of the secularization law was to divide the terrain among extant Mission Indians; however, Alta California locals or Californios were granted these plots. The cultivated rancho lands were utilized for cattle grazing, with an adobe-constructed residential unit established within twelve months of ownership. These conditional rancho grants were officially surveyed and marked by a handmade topological map.

Spain controlled California from 1776 to 1821 with primary intrigue in regional agricultural development. California land belonged to the king of Spain prior to the development of any ranchos. When Mexico became emancipated from Spain in 1822, the San Diego region became part of the Mexican democracy. Thus, California transitioned into a new epoch as a Mexican dependency with the closing of the mission period; ultimately, this opened the doorway to foreign trading.

California's American period was ushered in when California became a portion of the United States with the signing of the Treaty of Guadalupe Hidalgo. Territories had to be rationalized before a United States Land Commission as well as in the courts. The United States made sure that authentic California land titles would be esteemed. The San Diego region was augmented after the dissolution of the American-Mexican War by welcoming the arrival of various new people to California. These newcomers eventually altered the state's way of life.

Up until the mid-1850s, this land commission scrutinized these territories and diligently worked to determine the legal status of thousands of acres granted to private citizens. According to *Historic Ranchos of San Diego*, "Even under Spanish rule, California was a remote territory subject to little direct influence of the King or the Church. The revolution in Mexico brought independence to a new nation, and to California a further lessening of the always fragile ties of domination from Mexico City." Many difficulties developed for landowners and native peoples.

As we know, the rancho included vast unfenced zones of land, which included thousands of grazing cattle, sheep and horses. A substantial number of cowhides and tallow was produced at these ranchos, with cattle ultimately providing food, transportation and revenue prior to the 1848 discovery of gold in the state.

Prior to the arrival of Americans, Philip S. Rush, in his book *Some Old Ranchos and Adobes*, states:

> *Some writers have pictured life in the old rancho days as one long fiesta, enjoyed by gay caballeros and beautiful senoritas without a care or worry in the world. Such a picture is unrealistic. A very few rancheros were wealthy, and had beautiful haciendas. Many of them made pretense to affluence, while living in squalid adobe houses of one or two rooms without wooden floors, frequently with a cow hide for a door, no comfortable furniture, no heat, no running water, and sometimes with only the barest necessities to keep soul and body together. To such life could not have been glamorous, but it was what most of the people were accustomed to, in the years before the Americans came.*

The rancho lifestyle was an eclectic mix of hard work and leisure. Hunting, horse racing and bull and bear fights were common sports. The work of operating a rancho functioned as seamlessly as possible; there wasn't a rigid focus on class lines, as everyone, with the exception of the natives, had sufficient food and shelter. Rancho hospitality was at the forefront, as it was common to be cordial and welcoming to strangers. To take the mind away from day-to-day trials and tribulations, families and friends danced to the intricate steps of the fandango, jarabe and contradanza. Wedding balls typically lasted three or more days, with plenty of eating, drinking and dancing. Indeed, this early lifestyle was carefree and synonymous with one long, happy and fruitful holiday.

However, for the native peoples of that time, the rancho period was not as well received. The Indians were often coerced into being rancho servants. For the most part, they were not monetarily compensated for their work and were often dependent on the ranchos for necessary human needs, such as clothing, food, shelter and medical care. Sadly, they were extremely prone to developing disease due to unrelenting labor, unpleasant food, filthy accommodations and so on. There were strict punishments for any native person who voluntarily ran away from his or her rancho. Sadly, he or she was typically sought after and, upon return, reprimanded. In the coming chapters, you will read about Cave Johnson Couts, a bona fide legendary Southern California pioneer and sub-Indian agent who is as much imbedded in the state's historical tapestry as the rancho period itself.

The California gold rush directly affected the rancho period's prosperity. Indian life was forever interrupted when foreign people migrated to Southern California to strike it rich. Thousands of miners and those seeking opulence inundated Northern California. These new residents needed meat, thus increasing the demand for and price of cattle. For a time, gold deposits unearthed in California did provide new life for the rancho system; however, the stress induced from lawsuits and the influx of new people to the territory changed the lifestyle indefinitely: towns emerged, and there were also advances in agriculture. With the arrival of Americans, some of the immense holdings that had prevailed through the Land Commission and the weather were sold; with the advent of the 1880s, these portions of land were dismembered. From the mid-1950s to the mid-1960s, the rancho lands witnessed groundbreaking commercial and industrial development.

Sadly, many Southern California land ranchos have been forgotten and fallen into ruin over the past 150 years. In many ways, they open more doors for us to learn about the people who walked the land before us. Vista, California, is home to one of the last remaining land ranchos—one that has sustained the hands of time. Over the years, the legendary property would continue to be developed into what it is today. When you arrive at the black iron entrance gates on Alta Vista Drive and proceed down the historically lined brick walkway, you end at the ivy-laced courtyard door to the Rancho Buena Vista Adobe. Once you are there, you immediately sense the echoed vibrations from long ago. Indeed, this prized location is a bygone-era gem situated in the very heart of Vista. Southern California has a rich history, there's no doubt about it. There are numerous historic landmarks throughout San Diego and its northern communities, which serve as educational outposts for learning about the region's noted past. The Rancho Buena Vista is no exception.

Translated as "good view," the Rancho Buena Vista originally inhabited the western edge of an ancient Native American village. In fact, settlers from the early days documented portions of many standing adobe structures, which more or less became victims to time and rainy conditions. Upon total completion, the edifice stands as an L-shaped structure with portions extending north and east that connect to a beautifully landscaped courtyard. It is a single-story, Monterey-style building constructed of adobe brick walls, wooden ceilings and either tile or hardwood floors. Its square footage equals 4,189, with an additional board and batten kitchen, dining facility and pantry. The property was originally part of the landholdings of the Mission San Luis Rey. Along with the Mexican government's secularization

The beautiful Rancho Buena Vista Adobe courtyard where the lady in white has been spotted along the verandas. *Courtesy of Vista Historical Society*.

of California missions, the Rancho Buena Vista represented an 1845 land grant of around 2,200 acres.

The property was initially granted to Felipe Subria, a Luiseño Indian Mission San Luis Rey convert, by Mexico's governor Pio Pico. In 1846, Pio Pico came to the conclusion that California would soon no longer be under the auspices of Mexican control. Thus, he was broadminded in issuing grants to himself, his siblings and his friends. Born in 1801, Don Pio Pico spent his youthful years in San Diego. He was the Mission San Luis Rey's majordomo with the secularization of the missions. In 1841, Governor Juan Bautista Alvarado granted the 89,742-acre San Onofre and Santa Margarita rancho to Pico and his brother. Just three years later, the Pico brothers contracted the title to 43,699 acres affixed on the south from the native peoples who claimed it. This territory included some of the best grazing lands in all of Mission San Luis Rey's terrain. In 1845, Don Pio Pico fulfilled his desire to become the governor of Alta California.

San Luis Rey was the largest edifice in the entire mission system, made up of approximately three hundred miles. In 1834, when secularization came into effect, many native peoples settled in this attractive Southern California region. Subria had squatted on the Buena Vista lands until

1844, when Pio Pico ultimately granted him its 1,184 acres. According to Harrison and Ruth Doyle's book *A History of Vista*, during his tenure on the grounds, Subria "ran" horses, conducted some farming and built his tiny adobe house and three-sided horse stable near where the kitchen exists today. Legend holds that Subria was visited by the El Bandido Rojo, or the Red Bandit, who some believe was Joaquin Murietta or Tiburcio Vasquez, two men who were quite popular in the Southwest region. Intriguingly, bandit treasure of gold coins was reportedly stashed underneath the floorboards of one of the rooms inside the adobe; however, no such fortune was ever unearthed.

The adobe commenced as a shelter near Vista Creek and became the ultimate birthplace of the agricultural community of Vista, California. The city was once the hub of the surrounding California ranchos, being the center of cultural, economic and agricultural activities for over 140 years. The stories of the previous owners of the Rancho Buena Vista Adobe hail from diaries, old photographs and journals of Vista's longtime residents. Many legends have grown from the colorful history of these rancheros.

The "D" cattle brand is taken from some of the adobe's earliest owners, Maria La Gracia Subria Dunn—daughter of Felipe Subria, who deeded the rancho to her in 1850—and William Dunn. Maria wed American soldier William Dunn on August 22, 1851. As a wedding gift, Felipe offered the adobe and its land to the newlyweds for a mere sum of one dollar. It was Felipe's assertion that the couple continue to develop the land and care for him for the remainder of his days. Dunn became quite affluent during this time, amassing two acres of corn, one vineyard, a house, a corral, two wagons, nine horses, nine mares and colts, ten cows and more. Historical records suggest that Dunn wasn't the most honest man, as he resided with a Native American woman shortly after his marriage to Maria La Gracia. After accruing a substantial debt, he was coerced into deeding the property to a new owner, Jesus Machado.

The Dunns lost the property to its third proprietor, Machado, for a debt of eight dollars. Jesus was the son of Jose Manuel and Maria Serafina Valdez. Jesus wed Lugarda Alvarado in 1850, and at the time of their marriage, she had three sons and one daughter. While residing at their Buena Vista home, the newlyweds had two daughters and one son: Maria Felicita, Velizarda and Aloysius G., who went by the name of Luis. The Machado family was quite well known and influential throughout San Diego. In fact, many of Jesus's relatives ran various land grants. Like Dunn, he was quite intrigued with the idea of amassing wealth and becoming a landowner. It was during this time that the gold rush period began in the region, which helped Machado acquire money by selling cattle to miners.

At the time of receiving his Rancho Buena Vista land grant, Machado is credited with building a portion of the oldest adobe structure. He constructed his additional rooms in the Spanish style with two- to three-foot-deep walls and an overlapping thatch roof. Rugs enclosed the dirt floor, which was pounded flat to lessen the dust. Machado was very influential, as he developed the rancho's first irrigation system, making a dam out of the creek so he could have an annual basin of water. He produced orchards and enjoyed small-scale farming in addition to rearing farm animals. Sadly, he lost the title to the edifice for an alleged $800 debt in the 1860s, as a significant economic depression occurred during that time. Machado and his stepson Federico Alvarado traveled west and established land that connected the lines of the Agua Hedionda and Buena Vista ranches.

Next, the rancho thrived under the ownership of Lorenzo Soto, one of the last rancheros of the adobe and a renowned Los Angeles businessman and politician who made his fortune in the gold fields of Northern California. Born in 1821 in San Francisco, he possessed a lot of land spanning from San Luis Obispo to Old Town, San Diego. He, too, is credited with constructing other rooms at a right angle to the existing sizeable hacienda. The corner was intentionally left open so visitors could easily enter the premises. By 1860, his orchard consisted of twenty-six pear, three olive and several fig trees. Furthermore, he sold around twenty thousand hides from the San Jacinto area, thus accruing a lot of money. After the Civil War, Soto sold the land grant of over four thousand acres to Cave Johnson Couts and Ysidora Bandini de Couts for $3,000, a fair sum in 1866. Couts is credited with adding many rooms to the building, two verandas, orange trees and a substantial orchard.

As you will read in the upcoming chapters, the Couts family was a very prominent pioneer group in San Diego history. The elder Couts was a West Point graduate, becoming an army officer from Tennessee who traveled to San Diego and Mission San Luis Rey in 1848. After becoming one of the most affluent men in all of San Diego County, Couts controlled around twenty thousand acres of land and also held the title to Rancho Guajome, Rancho Vallecitos de San Marcos and Rancho Los Milipitos. Couts grazed 4,000 head of cattle, 340 horses, 56 mules and 550 sheep on his ranchos.

In the following year, the United States Census Bureau listed the official population of boomtown Vista as twenty-eight settlers and ten Indians. In 1876, after her husband's death, Ysidora Bandini de Couts gave the rancho as a wedding present to Maria Antonia and San Diego attorney Chalmers Scott, one of the founders of San Diego's Old Town. Chalmers Scott was educated in Europe and ranked at the top of his graduating class in the study of law at the University of New York. He then arrived in San Diego around 1870 and set up a joint law practice with Colonel G.A. Jones. A Protestant and thirty-second-degree Mason, he stipulated that any children from his marriage to Maria Antonia would be raised Catholic. In 1874, Scott wed Maria Antonia, the eldest daughter of Cave J. Couts and Ysidora Bandini de Couts, and became legal adviser to the Couts estate. The United States surveyor general examined the rancho in 1885 and deemed it to be 4,269 acres.

The Scotts were credited with remodeling the adobe by planting citrus orchards and vineyards while raising eleven children on the estate. As their fame and fortune grew, they moved to San Diego, and Maria deeded the rancho to her sister Dora (Ysidora Fuller Couts Gray) and her husband, Judge George Fuller, who had moved into the rancho in 1891. They added the board-and-batten kitchen and dining wing, making the hacienda a U-shaped structure. The Scotts' tenure at the adobe was carefree up until squatters settled on the property while Chalmers Scott was away in Arizona. In 1881, the squatters were ordered to vacate the premises but utilized the legal system to argue their right to stay on the land. They asserted that they were not in the original boundary lines of the rancho according to the land grant; thus, they had a legal right to stay. This commenced a series of legal entanglements for the Couts family members, and as a result, the U.S. General Land Office mandated the surveying of the Rancho Buena Vista for exact boundary lines. Boundary disputes and legal issues eroded the rancho holdings in the following year. Farmers settled on and claimed many zones within the grant declared by the Couts family. The courts favored one side over the other until the matter was decided in favor of the Couts family heirs in 1903. Ysidora Fuller and Couts Jr. were eventually granted one-fourth of the land, with the remaining land issued to various family members.

In regard to these land petitions, Craig Gilbert Bingley, in his 1993 master of arts thesis on the Rancho Buena Vista Adobe, stipulates, "In 1897, the Couts were awarded 1,109 acres and the rest of the land awarded to various settlers. Couts Jr., on behalf of the estate, petitioned to purchase the rest of the land. Ysidora Fuller and Couts Jr. disagreed on the distribution of the land awarded to the Couts family and the land to be purchased, so legal wrangling continued until 1903." Obviously, this was a source of great stress for the younger Ysidora, as many of her family

The passageway leading to the adobe's southern portion, as well as the dining room entrance on the left, circa 1990. *Courtesy of Alex Brandon.*

members, including herself, owed legal bills. Couts Jr. could not afford to pay all of his accrued debt, so he put the property into escrow. After George Fuller's passing on March 18, 1918, Ysidora Fuller sold her land to F. Jack Knight and his wife, Helen Louise, on September 21, 1919. She then relocated to Los Angeles. Over the course of eight years, Ysidora was paid $42,000 for the terrain and adobe property.

The Rancho Buena Vista Adobe was then subdivided as it went through the hands of various proprietors in the twentieth century. After Dora's husband passed away in 1918 on the premises of the Rancho Buena Vista Adobe, she borrowed significantly to maintain the property but, as we know, tragically lost it to a bank foreclosure in 1919. In the chapters to come, this book will discuss and highlight one of the spiritual legends associated with this rancho: the famed lady in white who graces the veranda inside the courtyard as well as the gallerias and gardens. This spirit is thought to be Ysidora Fuller Couts Gray.

Around 1912, the Vista Land Company obtained a considerable portion of the site and subsequently laid out some of the modern-day streets. With the arrival of World War I, the Rancho Buena Vista's acreage decreased to a mere fifty-one acres. When the rancho was purchased in 1919 by the Knights, the city of Vista had grown to a population of 350 residents. Helen Louise was an heir to a Colorado Cripple Creek goldmine. At the time of their purchase, the once expansive land had significantly depreciated. Many of the adobe's upgrades and conditions were completed in the 1920s by the Knights, who gave the City of Vista the adjacent Wildwood Park for all Vista residents to enjoy. They further modernized the pantry, dining room and kitchen in the 1920s. They also reinforced the roof and walls and revamped the kitchen to a more modern style.

Interestingly, the Vista Garden Club offered a reward to anyone who could come up with a unique name for the park. It was Lillie Electa Remsburg,

Left: The veranda space in front of the entrance to the majordomo room on the left where many visitors have seen the lady in white apparition. *Courtesy of Ali Schreiber.*

Right: When you visit the Rancho Buena Vista Adobe, make sure to take in the serenity by sitting at one of these tables while enjoying a coffee or tea. *Author's collection.*

wife of the *Vista Press* founder, who proposed the name "Wildwood Park," which has remained in existence ever since.

Hollywood came to Vista in 1931 with the arrival of MGM director Harry Pollard and his wife, silent-screen actress Margarita Fischer Pollard. Margarita remained at the adobe property after her husband's death, eventually selling it in 1957. In 1967, she was one of the founding directors of the Vista Ranchos Historical Society. Many celebrities visited the Pollards at the beautiful Rancho Buena Vista Adobe. Legend holds that the magnolia tree in the garden was gifted to the couple by actress Joan Crawford. The rancho was a dusty hilltop until the 1930s, when the Pollards commissioned Hollywood's Arthur Fields to create the gardens and enclosed courtyard. Today, the fountain provides a nice focal point in Fields's lush gardens.

Many photos during this period document the changes to the interior styles of the rancho. In fact, the Pollards dedicated $150,000 of their own money to restoring and revamping the adobe. Their renovations included

Escondido Avenue entrance to the Rancho Buena Vista Adobe. *Courtesy of Vista Historical Society.*

A unique shot of the L-shaped hacienda with the dining room entrance on the left and majordomo room entrance on the right. *Courtesy of Vista Historical Society.*

upgraded bathroom fixtures and large closets. They also hung heavy Europe-imported wooden doors in between rooms. Additionally, the couple installed a composition roof as a way to replace hand-hewn shingles, as well as a garage for their expensive vehicles. The tiles hailing from Italy, as seen in the bathroom, are some of the most aesthetically beautiful additions to the structure. The Pollards held ownership of the property for a respectable twenty years, until 1951.

In 1951, the rancho's 8.5 acres were sold to geologist and part-owner of the Las Vegas Golden Nugget Frederick Reid and his wife, Helen, for $85,000. Hailing from Toronto, the Reids actually utilized the Rancho Buena Vista as a summer home. They added modern carpet and furniture and adorned their adobe residence almost completely in white. Their chosen décor was French provincial and baroque. By this time, Vista's population had grown to five thousand residents.

After a six-year sojourn at the prized edifice, the Reids sold the adobe to Dr. Walter and Anastasia Weil for $100,000 in 1957. Dr. and Mrs. Weil rezoned

A sitting room in the Rancho Buena Vista Adobe's L-shaped hacienda, bordering the majordomo room, which is known for its paranormal encounters, circa 1957–1973. *Courtesy of Vista Historical Society.*

Anastasia Weil showcases a piece of her collected European artwork in the adobe's exquisite dining room, circa 1957–73. *Courtesy of Joe Rosenthal.*

the property and built a medical center with a pharmacy near the rancho's original Escondido Avenue entrance. Dr. Weil practiced ophthalmology there part time until he retired. He enjoyed reading and playing his violin in his spare time. Of course, they considered the adobe to be the epitome of uniqueness and value, so they decided to open up their property to the public

Anastasia Weil riding her bike on the Rancho Buena Vista property, circa 1957–73. *Courtesy of Vista Historical Society.*

for occasional house tours. With other residences added, these tours became a cherished annual event. The property needed a lot of tender loving care at the time they took over ownership of the Rancho Buena Vista. The orchard was neglected, and there were roof leaks and fifty-year-old plumbing.

To help remedy this situation, the family installed all copper piping and central heating. With an added swimming pool to offset the Southern California summer heat, they augmented the décor with artwork and artifacts from their travels around the world. Some of their collectibles included old Spanish paintings from the seventeenth century, early American maple chests and crucifixion scenes, as well as Mexican furnishings. The Weil family thus found the estate to be quite suitable for their massive collection of European antiques, furniture and oil paintings; however, they were coerced into selling the property in the early 1970s due to the significant amount of time needed to appropriately maintain the historic site. In March 1966, the Weils made a proposal to sell the property and surrounding terrain to the recently incorporated City of Vista. This viable opportunity remained open for half a year in 1968. Furthermore, at his own expense, Mr. Weil opted to construct a city administration complex on the Rancho Buena Vista property. With this agreement intact, the edifice was to be leased to the city with the intention of it taking over the rancho and subsequently utilizing it as a museum or historical site.

Craig Gilbert Bingley's master of arts thesis on the history of the Rancho Buena Vista Adobe asserts:

> *The city reviewed and calculated the costs of operation and on March 29, 1966 a meeting took place with Vista homeowners and the Chamber of Congress to highlight arguments in favor of public ownership of the property. All costs were analyzed, projected out and assessment of the condition of the current property, future buildings, needed repairs, etc. was provided.*

Now sealed up with cement, the former backyard pool is seen in this photograph. *Courtesy of Vista Historical Society*.

The Weils' family room featuring its vast collection of European artifacts, circa 1957–73. *Courtesy of Vista Historical Society*.

The sala grande's fireplace (seen here circa 1957–73) is still present today, and apparitional sightings have been spotted there. *Courtesy of Vista Historical Society.*

The annual cost of maintenance to the city was estimated to be $6,652 annually, the operating annual budget was $9,977, and immediate repairs totaled $28,396.

Sadly, Vista residents strongly opposed this offer, as they deemed it a waste of money. The townspeople felt that money should be reserved for maintaining streets and other city infrastructure. City council agreed to a vote, and on November 7, 1967, the proposal to buy the adobe and its lavish grounds was denied; thus, the Weils' options ran out, and they were coerced to put the property on the market.

In 1972, Rudd and Sally Schoeffel bought the house for $595,000, maintaining the historical character of the prized property by utilizing bricks constructed in the late 1800s from a historic edifice in Salt Lake City, Utah. They are also credited with adding the guesthouse and work done to plaster over the board-and-batten dining room. Additionally, they developed the Rancho Buena Vista Professional Center, as well as their 1981-constructed

An archway leading to the veranda on the adobe's southern side, where the root cellar is said to exist somewhere underneath the ground, circa 1957–73. *Courtesy Joe Rosenthal.*

restaurant, which further carried the adobe theme. Their ultimate goal was to blend additions in with the style of the original adobe structures by establishing three-foot-thick walls and deep-set windows and doorways.

In the early 1980s, the Schoeffels proposed to the city to transform the hacienda into a museum. Negotiations for this continued into 1986 as the City of Vista anticipated the state government's assistance would ultimately help with the museum. Due to rising real estate costs, the state ultimately denied assistance and left the city to fend for itself. The Schoeffels announced a new plan, which stipulated that the adobe would be torn down and its land rezoned for commercial purposes if the city did not purchase it. Ultimately, this was the momentum the city needed to purchase the adobe and its grounds at any cost. After the commencing of voter hearings, escrow was approved on July 10, 1989, for $1 million. Volunteers constructed the museum from scratch after the acquisition of the property. After thoughts of turning the site into a bed-and-breakfast, it was decided to utilize the legendary adobe for weddings and other events.

After the City of Vista purchased the property in 1989, many Vista residents made gifts to the rancho to provide the lovely furnishings that recall the historic depictions seen in the rooms today. The very north bedroom,

The picturesque courtyard fountain continues to serve as a focal point in modern times. *Courtesy of Vista Historical Society.*

also called the "stinky room," is believed to be the original structure built by Luis Machado in 1852. Its nickname comes from a story told by Cave Couts Jr. about the horse stable there and *el rojo bandito*, who coveted the stallion(s). With the addition of the sala grande, the adobe became a two-room house in the 1850s. The sala grande, or big living room, was the setting for prized entertainment. The master bedroom was added in the 1870s with Eastlake-style furniture and turn-of-the-century accessories. Italian tile, added by the Pollards, greatly updated the bathroom, the original carriage passageway into the courtyard.

Surely, by the 1850s, the Rancho Buena Vista Adobe was the focal point of the nearby ranches, having been the nucleus of cultural, economic and social festivities for over one hundred years. To date, it is the best preserved of the more than twenty-five original ranchos within San Diego County. Historians feel that this adobe in particular is the most safeguarded and genuine early California residence in modern-day existence.

EDUCATIONAL PROGRAMS AND EVENTS

The City of Vista's Parks and Community Services Department made the Rancho Buena Vista Adobe the center of its California Heritage Program. From Cinco de Mayo celebrations to art shows, guided tours and the Adobe Days education programs for third and fourth graders, all are opportunities for California residents and out-of-state visitors to learn about the rancho lifestyle and its heritage. Docents with the Friends of the Rancho Buena Vista Adobe are involved in many facets of preserving this historic rancho. Furthermore, many couples choose to tie the knot at the adobe, as it offers a beautiful outdoor ambience for their special day.

One of the guest house rooms where our Spirits of the Adobe tour guests watch an educational video about the Rancho Buena Vista Adobe. *Author's collection.*

It is our honor that proceeds from Spirits of the Adobe tours directly benefit the parks and community services department and further restoration of the legendary site. The San Diego Paranormal Research Society (SDPRS) has been conducting these fundraising haunted history tours since 2011. After initial introductions at the start of the event, guests watch a short, well-produced video about the adobe's history. We also discuss how we utilize our equipment arsenal prior to heading inside the adobe's rooms. Once inside the L-shaped structure, guests have the opportunity to collaborate with us on paranormal experimentation, including a dowsing rod session in the kitchen, spirit box session in the majordomo room and live electronic voice phenomena session in the sala grande. Of course, we take attendees through each space inside the adobe as well so they can see the European artifacts and historical photographs and hear about what life was like during the Rancho Buena Vista's heyday.

An Introduction to the Adobe's Paranormal Activity

Humans have always been instinctively intrigued with the concept of life after death. Many cultures exhibit some form of belief in the paranormal. In recent years, this collective drive to understand ghosts and spirits has skyrocketed exponentially as inherent interest in studying the afterlife has infiltrated our very core of existence. Since the dawning of time, many folks have been on an everlasting quest to examine, discover and hopefully answer the pervading questions that exist around the supernatural realm: "What are ghosts and spirits?" "How does human consciousness survive death?" "Where exactly do we all go once our bodies cease to function in the mortal realm?" "Are spirits actually communicating with the living?" "If so, how do they do so?"

Historical events and paranormal phenomena share a deep kinship; you really can't have one without the other. When a location is deeply embedded in history, it's really no wonder how and why supernatural events occur there. Of course, paranormal events cannot be proven or yet completely understood by scientific standards; however, history and ghostly happenings are quite intertwined, best friends with a dear kinship. Thus, you really cannot have one without the other, as a site's times gone by are the foremost reason why it has ghosts, spirits and strange occurrences.

There are other theoretical hypotheses about the cause of hauntings at certain places that can partially explain a site's supernatural events, so it's really a matter of examining all of the prevailing theories and seeing how they fit in with the overall historical tapestry of a notable location. No person can completely comprehend a location's haunting without looking into the intricacies of its past. Thorough paranormal research teams, such as the San Diego Paranormal Research Society, spend countless hours digging through historical archives as a way to understand a site's past and connect the pieces of its biographical puzzle. We can conclude that paranormal research allows us to viscerally be placed in a past epoch among the once-living individuals that exist as spirits in modern time.

Southern California is steeped in a complex historical narrative; thus, it is no wonder that it's reckoned as one of the most supernaturally active regions in the United States and beyond. California's rancho period is said to have spanned the length of one hundred years, so imagine all of the stories amassed over that time. The rancho period is one of the most talked about and studied times in all of California history. In 1846, by the time of the termination of Mexican rule in California, these land parcels covered millions of acres. Proprietors of these expansive land grants were not only quite affluent, but they were also the chief leaders in politics and social life.

Indeed, the "golden era" of the rancho period was immersed in a lifestyle that promoted fiestas, laughter, wealth and leisure amid the hardships that came with running a thriving plot of land. Therefore, a lot of joy as well as a lot of sorrow infiltrated many of these ranchos, leaving a psychic imprint today where visitors can viscerally sense what life was like many years ago. Places that have been witness to a plethora of emotions are said to be more susceptible to hauntings and paranormal occurrences—another abounding theory about why many Southern California ranchos are deeply rooted in ghostly happenings.

When you study the historical timeline of the Rancho Buena Vista Adobe owners, you can immediately construe how populated the location was for several years. Indeed, this adobe housed an eclectic mix of individuals, from early Native Americans and San Diego pioneers to Hollywood moguls and extremely wealthy individuals—people from various walks of life and differing backgrounds. Somehow, their times gone by can be viscerally felt and sensed in modern times; thus, the veil between our world and the afterlife becomes more perceptive and tangible. When this happens, authentic study of the spiritual world occurs.

Above: The east-facing veranda where the lady in white is occasionally spotted, circa 1957–73. *Courtesy of Vista Historical Society*.

Left: The Rancho Buena Vista Adobe's front veranda, which also serves as an entrance to the sala grande, circa 1957–73. *Courtesy of Vista Historical Society*.

Another view of the south-facing veranda that highly depicts Spanish architecture, circa 1957–73. *Courtesy of Vista Historical Society.*

In our seven-plus years of conducting paranormal study on the Rancho Buena Vista Adobe's premises, we have documented a wide range of spiritual occurrences that can be experienced by all of the five human senses. From visual and auditory encounters to being touched by unseen hands to the pervasive feeling that you're being watched by invisible eyes, the adobe has it all. The energies are friendly, curious and willing to communicate with those who demonstrate a genuine intrigue about their story. So take a seat and enjoy reading about the haunted history of Vista's iconic landmark. When you visit its premises, you may have an encounter with one of its beloved spirits.

CHAPTER 2

GHOSTLY HIGHLIGHTS AT THE RANCHO BUENA VISTA ADOBE

Although supernatural events can arise at any given moment and in any given location at the legendary rancho, there are specific "hot spot" spaces within the L-shaped structure that are more susceptible to ghostly goings-on. These particular rooms include the majordomo room, sala grande and kitchen. Other rooms are known to produce a variety of ghostly encounters as well; however, these three locations within the structure are more consistently inundated with spiritual phenomena. In the coming chapters, you will read about more specific sightings and encounters that occur within the walls of these rooms.

For now, let's focus on the types of supernatural occurrences that the Rancho Buena Vista is known for. Visual and auditory phenomena are the most prolific types of paranormal activity at this historic location; paranormal researchers from the San Diego Paranormal Research Society have been consistently documenting both types throughout their years studying this celebrated locale. In fact, a former City of Vista employee showed me an iconic photo of what looked like three spiritual humanoid shadow forms standing in the middle of the historic lined brick walkway, which leads into the property off Alta Vista Drive. The photo was captured by another San Diego–based paranormal research team.

Another commonality among guests' encounters with the adobe's spirits isn't so much tangible as it is a sixth sense that an invisible someone is with you. There have been numerous occasions when people reported the feelings of being watched by unseen eyes. It's a rather unique experience, and you'll

The brick walkway space in between the L-shaped structure and the guest house on the right. *Author's collection.*

The current entrance to the Rancho Buena Vista Adobe from Alta Vista Drive originally established by the Schoeffels. *Courtesy of Vista Historical Society.*

know when you encounter it. Furthermore, it's one of the most frequently sensed supernatural vibrations at haunted sites.

Along these lines enters an experience reported by Frank Rojano in regard to one of the caterers during a July 2008 wedding. He goes on to impart this caterer's psychic senses while working on the property and managing the Louisiana barbecue–style menu. Frank goes on to share how this wedding staff member came up to him, asking, "Does this place have any history? Has anyone noticed any funny things?" Of course, in a matter-of-fact tone, Frank answered him in the affirmative. Apparently, the caterer disclosed how he can pick up spirit energy and was sensing quite a bit at the adobe. Being the kind person that he is, Frank decided to give the employee a tour of the hacienda. When they arrived at the master bedroom, the man's psychic senses were quite elevated as he exclaimed, "The energy right here is so strong." The room turned cold, while the adjacent sala remained warm, as it was a hot summer day. The freezing cold spot followed them as they traversed through the remainder of the rooms.

To date, partially and fully manifested ghostly forms have appeared in almost every single room inside the adobe. The dining room and kitchen space was added on by Ysidora Fuller Couts Gray and her husband, Judge George Fuller. We take guests through both of these areas on our tours; we've dedicated much time to both areas on private paranormal investigations as well. Several individuals have documented seeing a short lady adorned in vintage attire walk straight into a storage closet that is set off the main kitchen. We have a prevailing theory for the cause of this particular specter. An electronic security system exists on the inside wall of the storage space, which emits electromagnetic frequencies, or EMF. Since EMF is theorized to be a capacitor for spiritual energy, we think it may be charging this particular female entity. If she is residual in origin, such as a psychic imprint on the environment, then electricity has no bearing on her manifestation.

During a paranormal research event with just three San Diego Paranormal Research Society members, we all encountered some ethereal existence while conducting an audio session inside the main kitchen. All of a sudden, we heard a seemingly disembodied whistling sound emanating from the actual dining room. A tall shadow figure was also seen entering through the entrance to the dining room. Whenever you can have two or more experiences or captured evidence, more pieces of the paranormal puzzle are connected, further indicating that the encounters are closer to being supernatural in origin. Being the productive investigator that she is, my co-investigator Ali Schreiber decided to make sure that our security personnel

The kitchen space is used for school-aged educational programs and is also the prime location for the divining rod experiment during our Spirits of the Adobe tours. *Author's collection.*

wasn't outside in the courtyard area and could possibly have been mistaken for the spotted shadow figure. After careful scrutiny, we determined that the security team wasn't anywhere near the vicinity of where we were, thus making the incorporeal sounds and sightings all the more elusive.

Knocking sounds and the noises of disembodied footsteps are two auditory encounters inside the dining room and kitchen space that have been recorded on more than one occasion. During the Spirits of the Adobe tours, we educate guests in the kitchen on how to properly conduct a dowsing (divining) rod session. Four or five rhythmic knocking sounds were heard emanating from the right side of the kitchen on two separate occasions. After careful examination, we were able to replicate the exact noises when tapping on the kitchen door's windowpanes and could determine where the sounds came from. There was no one outside the door, as our security guard was inside the guesthouse, which is located outside the arched courtyard gateway. Both adobe entrance gates are locked once all tour attendees come on site, so we ruled out the possibility that a transient individual came inside the property.

We have documented some intriguing movement with the rods during our time spent in the kitchen. On a few occasions, they have seemingly pointed to a certain space within the kitchen when we've asked, "Can you point the rods to where you are located inside the room?" We've also asked, "Can you point one or both rods where Nicole or Ali is standing?" Sure enough, on quite a few occasions, this is exactly what occurred. A spirit by the name of Juan Gonzalez as well as the ethereal energy of Ysidora Bandini de Couts seem to enjoy communicating with guests via the divining instruments. Claire, one of the late docents who devoted a lot of effort to the Rancho Buena Vista Adobe, has also preferred to interact with guests via the rods. We've done some experimentation where we've asked the adobe spiritual residents to manipulate the rods by asking them if they were present with us. For example, we have inquired, "Juan, if you are here with us, can you cross the rods?" We then asked the same question for all of the intelligent, interactive spirits of the adobe and have had the dowsing rods cross for certain ethereal energies.

Claire and her husband, Clarence, were very instrumental in pushing the City of Vista to acquire the Rancho Buena Vista Adobe and establish its museum space. She had a profound love for the property and would often sit outside the guesthouse in complete awe. Frank Rojano shared that he was trained by Claire, so he discovered some of her likes, such as the site's indigenous plants and flowers. A dedication memorial for both Claire and Clarence exists along the property's north pathway that borders Wildwood Park. This is a great commemoration for the two of them, a permanent reminder of their relentless devotion to Vista's iconic site.

Claire loved the adobe so much that perhaps she continues to make appearances there in spirit form. We have had some intriguing divining rod sessions with Claire, as she seems drawn to utilizing them. A few years ago, the son of a retired City of Vista employee joined us on our Spirits of the Adobe tours. He knew Claire quite well, so he asked her some questions during a collective group ethereal communication session in the sala grande. He went on to say, "Claire, if you are here, can you show me a sign?" Almost immediately after, one of our devices said the name "Claire." Needless to say, there were quite a few gasps among the living!

Added on by the Pollards during their tenure at the site, the guesthouse is located across the arched L-shaped adobe structure's entrance gate. Fascinating encounters have occurred here. In 2011, the San Diego Paranormal Research Society conducted its premiere paranormal investigation at the Rancho Buena Vista Adobe. We spent the first couple of

A memorial bell commemorating the work of beloved Rancho Buena Vista Adobe docent Claire and her husband, Clarence. *Courtesy of Ali Schreiber.*

hours inside the guesthouse and experienced some otherworldly phenomena. The moon provided soft lighting through the windows, as the lights inside were completely shut off. Within a few minutes, we heard the shuffling sounds of someone walking inside the space. There were two of us present during this project, and we were sitting down at the time. Disembodied whisper vocalizations were heard throughout the time we spent inside the guesthouse—residual reminders of times gone by.

We were pleasantly surprised when we examined our audio, photographs and video surveillance a few days after our supernatural research project. A disembodied voice of "guests" was captured on one of the static cameras placed in the guesthouse kitchen, not to be confused with the one that's inside the L-shaped adobe structure. There's a captivating backstory to this particular audio capture: about two seconds prior, an investigator opened the guest home's front entrance doors as she was walking in from the outside. Thus, the spirit vocalization of "guests" indicates some intelligence; it's almost as though this spirit said "guests" as a way to announce that he or she was aware of a living person opening the front entrance door.

Visual phenomena have recently spiked inside the guesthouse, specifically in the gathering spaces where the monthly art displays are held. This is the area where we commence our Spirits of the Adobe tours; we set up a table full of equipment and gadgets commonly utilized for paranormal research. Ethereal misty forms and simultaneous cold spots have occurred on several occasions. Humanoid shadow forms have been spotted darting about the area in visitors' peripheral vision. Is it possible that these wraithlike forms enjoy the presence of living individuals, as they seemingly occur more often when the guesthouse is populated? Perhaps they are quite familiar with our monthly tour routine and stop by to acknowledge our attendance. Original 1850 bricks and *morteros*, rock-carved holes that the native peoples used to grind nuts and seeds, are situated at the bottom of the fireplace in the main front room of the guesthouse. Is it possible that spiritual residue is attached to these historic items and they are the source of some of the paranormal activity here?

Frank Rojano has worked for the City of Vista for many years. He has also accompanied us on our Spirits of the Adobe tours many times. He is often by himself at the adobe during the night and has mentioned that he isn't afraid of the energies there. In his own words, he shares some captivating personal experiences he's encountered in the guesthouse (gallery):

For me, I get the feeling that it's a male energy in here. He hasn't talked, but it's just a feeling. My first experience in here was when I became a park director when on weekends, they would call us for any alarm calls. Since I was on duty, I received a call that the alarm in the gallery went off. It was about 1:00 a.m. or 2:00 a.m. when I was alerted that one of the alarms in the adobe was going off in the guesthouse. When I inquired as to how it was set off, the alarm company's representative said, "Let me see here." She got back on the phone saying that someone pushed the panic button. So, somebody had to have pushed the ambulance button.

The cops had already gone there to check on things, as they automatically go there after an alarm goes off. Of course, they just walked the perimeter, as the building was locked. The cops didn't find anything wrong, and I was told that I had to go to the adobe to reset the alarm. So, I am close by, so I got there in five minutes. The sheriff was just leaving and said that everything looked fine, as there were no broken windows, no strange people around, so it must have been some sort of malfunction. I opened the door and the closet where the alarm is. Thinking that something fell inside the

A front view of the Rancho Buena Vista Adobe's guesthouse entrance. *Author's collection.*

closet, I started looking around. But everything that was in the closet was below the line of the alarm, so there was nothing high enough to fall. So I wrote this experience off as a malfunction.

I double-checked all the windows to make sure they were locked. Everything looked good. As I was getting ready to lock the main door and reset the alarm, the door to the washroom by the kitchen slammed. That's the door where we have a little rock by it, as it tends to slowly move and shut. It doesn't really slam, but it slowly closes. Of course, I had to apply some logical thinking to try and explain this. So, I reopened the door and put the little rock down at the bottom, and as I went back to reset the alarm again—I was just about to set it—the door slams again, and that little round rock just rolled down the hallway, hit and bounced off the wall a little bit. So I reset the alarm and got out of there. This was my first experience in this guesthouse gallery.

In his own words, Frank goes on to share his second experience in the guesthouse gallery:

The second experience occurred when we had an artist bring in Indian-themed paintings. We just had an artist reception, and there were people leaving, so I was going to close up after everybody left. There were a couple of ladies still there who were looking at the pictures, so I waited for them. I was on the other side of the room in the dining area by the door that leads into the kitchen. Near the cubbies, there were two little small easels that had pictures of Indians. The right-sided one had a painting of an Indian's face. In front, there were two easels, one with Elvis Presley pictures and the other with Marilyn Monroe pictures. While I was looking at them, the picture of the Indian head on my right side flew across the room all the way to the other side by the French doors. It breaks as it hits the corner of the wall. Of course, I had to report this, as we have insurance.

Continuing on, Frank shares his third experience in this particular space:

About 2005 or 2006, my boss called me one time and wanted to know if I wanted to earn double pay, as a family wanted to rent the main hacienda's old dining room for Thanksgiving dinner. It was going to be catered, so the only thing I had to do was open the gallery (guesthouse) so they could use the restroom as well as the dining room, as it was the only room they were going to use. So people start coming; the caterer came and started setting up.

The main space in the guesthouse where we commence our Spirits of the Adobe tours. *Author's collection.*

I let everyone know that I was going to be in the other house (guesthouse). I had to be there for about three hours. I walked around to the back wall where the guesthouse fountain is. From outside, I could see through the French doors to the main entrance door. I could see the bride's room through the French doors and the dining room through the other set of doors. I figured that if someone comes to use the bathroom, I could see them enter the guesthouse. So I am sitting in the back, as it was a nice night. After a few minutes of being outside, I happened to look as the bride's room television was on. I figured that somebody must have come inside and turned it on, but I didn't see anyone. So I go in the guesthouse, and the lights were off in the bathroom. It didn't look as though anyone entered the premises, so I turned the TV off. I walk outside to the backyard again, and by the time I got outside, I noticed that the television was on again! This time, I knew that no one came inside, as I just checked and the front door was closed. This time, I go back inside yet again and unplugged the TV.

Of course, there's no real way to prove that Frank's encounters were completely paranormal in origin. He was smart to apply logical and sensible thinking as a way to try to rationally explain his peculiar experiences. He couldn't quite produce a common-sense reason for what caused his

Another shot of the Rancho Buena Vista Adobe's dining room, originally constructed by Ysidora Couts Gray and her husband, George Fuller, circa 1970s. *Courtesy of Vista Historical Society.*

seemingly otherworldly happenings, so he deemed them as potential supernatural incidents. These events also showcase how ghostly phenomena can apparently be strong enough to move objects. These psychokinetic effects often occur at locations steeped in active hauntings.

Big enough for a small bedroom, the bathroom inside the L-shaped structure is the most aesthetically appealing of any historic property we've been to. Imported by the Pollards from Italy, gorgeous tile covers the bathtub and double vanity sink, along with European toiletry artifacts. One of the most enchanting encounters to date at the Rancho Buena Vista Adobe happened during our very first Spirits of the Adobe tour. As the tour hosts and guests were situated inside the bathroom, we shared the pertinent history pertaining to this luscious lavatory. As we were doing so, all of us heard the sound of something dragging across the tiled floor. Immediately, our investigator mode kicked in, and we started to move certain objects as a way to replicate the noise. When we moved the vanity's small white stool, we immediately discovered the exact sound we had heard moments before. So we determined that the stool moved seemingly of its own volition, as we ruled out the likelihood of anyone living accidentally bumping into it. The natural settling of the building was definitely not strong enough to move an object as heavy as this precise stool, nor was a typical California earthquake, should it have occurred. Therefore, we have chalked up this event to another mysterious occurrence in the chapter of paranormal phenomena at the Rancho Buena Vista.

The gathering room, also known as the family room, lies adjacent to the bathroom on the northern side of the building. One of the most common claims of this space has to do with a formerly hung mirror on the west-end wall between the two shuttered windows. Many visitors to the adobe have documented seeing a man's face with a beard that vanishes as quickly as it appears in the mirror. Witnesses have described his features as being round and heavy, with a beard. Now, Maria Antonia, the eldest daughter of the Coutses, was married to Chalmers Scott, who strikingly matched this image. After scrutinizing this mirror, there are no permanent smudges or scratches

A modern-day view of the double vanity sink bathroom renovated by the Pollards. In earlier times, this space served as a passageway for carriages. *Author's collection.*

Known as the gathering room, this space features some of the finest displays of European architecture in the entire structure. *Author's collection.*

that someone could matrix into the likes of a person's face. Currently, a hutch stands where the mirror hung on the wall.

Another mysterious encounter happened in this room during our very first paranormal research project at the adobe. There were only two of us present, which ruled out possible human contamination of personal encounters or collected evidence. A disembodied male child's voice was heard while an investigator was comfortably seated on the steps bordering the family room and original small adobe space. We could not decipher the words that were spoken, but we clearly determined that it came from a small boy. At the time of this experience, only a basic understanding of the Rancho Buena Vista Adobe's historical narrative was known. However, after spending seven-plus years acquiring a substantial amount of information pertaining to this historic site, we strongly suspect that we heard the otherworldly vocalization of either William Couts or Robert Lee Couts, Cave and Ysidora's younger sons, whom you will read more about in later pages.

Now, here's where it becomes more mysterious: you see, both William and Robert passed away when they were adults; however, we have possible

56

paranormal evidence of them coming through as children. In the spirit world, it is theorized that certain earthbound entities and/or spirits choose to come through in ethereal form as children; perhaps their youthful days were happier and filled with more positivity compared to when they were adults. Then again, we also believe in the probability of both William and Robert spiritually manifesting in both adult and child form, depending on the circumstances.

The original adobe room or "stinky room," a name given by Cave Couts Jr., quietly sits as a reminder of the earliest days in Rancho Buena Vista's history. We typically end our Spirits of the Adobe tours in this space while offering guests a chance to practice psychometry, or the ability to acquire sensations or impressions while holding or touching an object. There are original 1850s bricks that we utilize for this experiment. Phantom olfactory senses have been documented by several of our guests, as well as shadow-figure sightings permeating the room's doorway.

A few servants' quarters exist on the Rancho Buena Vista Adobe's south side. These are located just east of where the pool used to be and are utilized for educational programs. We don't have time to take guests through these areas during our Spirits of the Adobe tours, but we have spent some time in each room during private research projects. These quarters are known to produce supernatural activity just as much as the main L-shaped structure does.

During an investigation in 2014, a few investigators were seated at a large round table for a spirit communication session. We had various gadgets scattered across the table that are designed for measuring environmental fluctuations. Almost immediately, we were all tapping into both male and female disembodied voices, as well as extreme cold spots. At one point, we heard a youthful-sounding female vocalization emanate through our device, saying, "Hi." Then, a few minutes later, as we were all talking among ourselves, two different disembodied voices came through saying, "Hi… hi." Immediately, we wondered if two spiritual entities were conversing with each other. Needless to say, it was quite interesting.

As we continued on with our research for the night, one of the investigators facing east suddenly felt ice-cold on his back. This particular project took place during a warm summer night, and without air conditioning in the room, we couldn't immediately explain the cold spot. A few moments after he documented feeling chilled, another researcher spotted an ethereal figure standing behind him. This specter wasn't fully manifested but appeared in a dark gray silhouette. It hovered behind the investigator for just a couple of

For years, people have walked through this iconic arched gateway leading to the spacious courtyard. *Courtesy of Vista Historical Society.*

seconds before vanishing. Was this the spirit form of one of the Couts family members? Or was a spirit by the name of Juan Gonzalez curious as to what we were doing in the servants' quarters on this bright moonlit night?

The past stories, accounts and memories of the entire L-shaped adobe structure, as well as its adjacent land, continue to pulsate in the present. Walls really do talk at the Rancho Buena Vista Adobe, as the entire renowned landmark is alive with presence. There are so many visitors to the adobe who report unusual happenings within its confines on a consistent basis. The San Diego Paranormal Research Society is duly honored to be the official host of the Spirits of the Adobe tours and the only team to have spent over seven years conducting extensive historical and paranormal research into this prized Vista landmark. We keep meticulous notes and records pertaining to our collected research and paranormal evidence.

To date, the Rancho Buena Vista Adobe is an ongoing historical and paranormal research project for the San Diego Paranormal Research Society. When we started our private investigations and Spirits of the Adobe tours at the legendary hacienda, we did not yet realize the profound impact it was going to make not only on ourselves but also on our outlook on the supernatural. Indeed, our experiences with its ethereal residents have taught us so much about the supernatural realm. For that, we are forever grateful. Our research of the adobe has further supported our belief in life after death. There are just too many mysterious incidents that occur within the confines of the Rancho Buena Vista Adobe to be labeled anything other than paranormal. We look forward to many more years at this iconic and beautiful Vista location.

CHAPTER 3

THE LEGEND OF THE MAJORDOMO ROOM

The term *majordomo* is used to describe the head foreman's space within a rancho site. The majordomo room in the Rancho Buena Vista Adobe is a small area decorated in a western fashion with an actual horse saddle, rawhide materials and an antique desk. It is located in the center portion of the adobe, constructed along with two other rooms by Lorenzo Soto after he purchased the property in 1856. Soto added the spaces at a right angle to the existing structure using the same adobe construction methods. The buildings did not connect; however, the corner of the structure was left wide open and utilized as an entrance to the grounds.

The majordomo room is small, approximately twenty feet by twenty feet, with a small vanity area consisting of a sink adorned with beautiful Italian tile. There is a window looking south toward the rear garden area and another window looking east, offering a view of the breezeway between the adobe's living quarters and kitchen and dining room. The majordomo room is also located adjacent to the children's room, named because it was originally the bedroom of Maria Antonia's offspring. It was used as a bedroom by other proprietors as well.

We conduct our spirit communication session within the majordomo confines during our monthly Spirits of the Adobe tours; we are proud to say that we've consistently acquired profound, historically relevant and contextual responses to our line of questioning when conversing with the ethereal beings at this rancho. Over the course of seven years, Ali Schreiber and I have asked the ghostly energies questions pertaining to

Looking out onto the courtyard veranda from the majordomo room, where we conduct a spirit communication session during our Spirits of the Adobe tours. *Author's collection.*

the historical tapestry of the Rancho Buena Vista with surprising results. Additionally, at times, we have acquired captivating communication and/ or responses to our questions that we've been able to verify by examining historical archives of the historic site.

Electric wiring was installed in the early 1930s at the Rancho Buena Vista Adobe. What an electrician discovered in the majordomo room one day will leave anyone's hairs standing straight up for some time. While ripping open the adobe walls to set up electricity, a man's skeleton was found hanging lifelessly by a rope. While there is no official documentation to prove this, supposedly the electrician was fearful of disturbing the remains. Thus, the wall was sealed back up. It is the wall between this space and the children's room that is thought to house these remains. Perhaps it is one of the main reasons for much of the paranormal activity many individuals encounter when stepping foot on adobe grounds.

So, we are left to wonder, is there still a skeleton within this wall? And if so, what is the identity of the person believed to be entombed in the

A portion of the majordomo room where human skeletal remains were said to be found by an electrician during the late 1920s or early 1930s. *Author's collection.*

wall of the majordomo room, and how did he or she get there? Although many theories abound, paranormal investigators believe that the remains may belong to an Indian named Juan Gonzalez who worked on the property many years ago. We have collected evidence, especially during the past four years, that suggests that the legend of Juan Gonzalez may, in fact, be true. In the past few years, both Ali and I have obtained a plethora of paranormal evidence in the form of audio communication, highly suggesting that these human bones indeed belonged to a man by this name.

Juan's origins are quite elusive; we really don't know where he came from. We believe that he may have belonged to the Luiseño Native American tribe based on some intriguing historical information in regard to the 1850 Act for the Government and Protection of Indians. According to Michael Magliari in his article "Free Soil, Unfree Labor: Cave Johnson Couts and the Binding of Indian Workers in California, 1850–1867," a portion of this statute legalized the process of acquiring Native American workers as "bound prisoners, custodial wards, or later, as indentured 'apprentices.'" Section 3 permitted employers to be granted custody of Native American offspring, rearing them until they reached the age of majority, more specifically, eighteen years for males and fifteen for females. Employers were mandated to obtain the consent of a child's parents or friends, joining them in front of a justice of the peace who was responsible for issuing a certificate of custody. Section 4 necessitated certificate holders to take care of the Indian wards by clothing and feeding them, as well as instituted fines for any inhumane treatment.

From 1850 to 1865, this Indian act played an important role in sustaining the rancho lifestyle and economic atmosphere. After spending seven-plus years researching the Rancho Buena Vista Adobe, we stumbled upon some additional information that sheds a light on Juan's background and further supports the notion that he was an indentured servant to Ysidora Bandini de Couts. In April 1854, Governor John Bigler appointed Cave J. Couts to the San Diego County Court, where he functioned on the county's Court of Sessions. Just twelve months later, Judge Couts represented the San Luis Rey township while on the county board of supervisors. During the mid-1800s, the elder Couts held other noteworthy positions, including justice of the peace, judge of the plains and federal Indian sub-agent. Taking advantage of the Indian act of 1850, Couts bought many Indian children while issuing legal custody to his wife, Ysidora.

In January 1854, Cave and Ysidora obtained an Indian female child named Sasaria from Jesus and Paula Delgado, who were two of Couts's employees. Furthermore, they acquired custody of Juan, an Indian boy of ten to twelve years of age, and custody was transferred to Ysidora in April 1855. There are several mentions of a man by the name of Juan linked to Ysidora in Cave Johnson Couts's many journals and registers held at the Huntington Library in San Marino, California. The book *The American Italy: The Scenic Wonderland of Perfect Climate* mentions how a small boy by the name of Juan Asis was given to Cave J. Couts around 1856; this boy went by the last name of Couts until 1873, when he was incarcerated for stealing a horse. Consequences ensued, and Juan Asis was mandated to go by the name of "Couche." Even more compelling was how his father, Pablo Asis, once owned the Rancho Guajome, the other noted historic site that once belonged to the famed Couts family.

Another variation highlights the possibility that the Juan in question was actually a man by the name of Juan Diego, who was murdered for horse theft. What's captivating about this hypothesis is how we have uncovered clues to the root cellar that was located behind the L-shaped adobe structure. We were able to take some spirit communication results and verify them by examining genuine historical archives. What we discovered indicates the strong possibility of Cave Couts Jr. imprisoning horse thieves and other individuals in this particular underground crypt.

On one of our research nights at the adobe, we directly asked if livestock was stored in this subterranean vault, at which point we obtained a spirit response of "men." We also inquired as to how many people were kept in this space, acquiring a firm response of "four" just seconds later. Even more was revealed when one of our guests asked, "Were you one of the men kept down there?" A male response strikingly similar to Juan's vocal

Many people have sensed feelings of sadness along the confines of this back veranda, possibly correlating to the underground root cellar where some individuals were imprisoned during the adobe's earlier years. *Courtesy of Ali Schreiber.*

tone came through, answering "yes." To be extra sure, Ali then asked, "Juan, it's Ali. Were you ever kept down there?" A whispered response immediately breaks through, answering, "I was down there."

Continuing on with our very sensitive audio session, we then asked to know the names of some of the other men who were detained in the cellar. The names that we heard were Juan and Herman Diaz, who worked for Cave J. Couts. As if this session couldn't get any more emotional and heart-wrenching, we made one last query by asking, "Was it Cave Couts Sr. or Cave Couts Jr. that incarcerated the men in the cellar?" A confident response of "son" was heard just seconds after. It was at this point that tears were shed and we offered a positive and peaceful affirmation to the spiritual energies that experienced the horrific times of being locked away in the ground. I openly shared with the spirits that they do not have to relive any pain, anxiety, suffering or torture that occurred as a result of being locked away. I went on to say, "You are free of that," at which point a spirited vocalization came through saying "*Sí*," or "yes" in Spanish. Paranormal evidence, even as striking and revealing as it can be at times, still isn't considered concrete proof. However, authenticity reigns when one can verify spirit communication by linking it with actual historical information.

Following is the actual transcript of the aforementioned sensitive communication session:

August 16, 2016

Nicole: The outside tunnel out there, was that used as a root cellar or was it used to keep prisoners there? Can you confirm and clarify for us please?

Spirit response: Two consecutive whispers saying "kept."

Nicole: So we know that something was kept down there, so can you clarify whether there was food or were there people kept there?

Nicole: Was it used as a jail?

Ali: Did you keep any type of livestock down there, such as goats or sheep?

Spirit response: "men"

Nicole: That's very valuable information. Thank you so much. We really appreciate it.

Nicole: Just one more question about that: how many men at one time were kept down there? One or two or more than two?

Spirit response: "More" and "Yes."

Nicole: Can you tell us, sir, what your name is? We are so sorry that you were kept down there.

Nicole: What is your name, sir? It is okay, you don't have to be afraid to tell us, we just want to know.

Ali: Juan, it's Ali. Were you ever kept in that cellar?

Spirit response: "Yes, I was down there."

Nicole: We don't want to force you to answer.

Ali: It could be another Juan.

Nicole: It could be another Juan, right.

Nicole: Can you tell us the names of some of the other men who were kept down there? Do you know their names?

Spirit response: "Herman." (There is a photo of a Herman Diaz in the majordomo room.)

Nicole: Herman Diaz, I am so sorry if you were kept down there.

Ali and tour guest: We both heard "Diaz" through the device.

Nicole: I did, too.

Nicole: Herman, we are so, so sorry. We are so, so sorry. And I do want to let you know, Herman, and this goes for all the men who were unfortunately kept down there, you don't have to relive that pain anymore.

Spirit response: "I know."

Tour guest: I have one more question, and I have to ask this question: is the man in the wall someone who was kept in the cellar?

Spirit response: "Yes."

Tour guest: I am so, so sorry.

Ali: And we believe that person to be Juan Gonzalez? Is that correct?
Spirit response: "Yes."
Ali: Who kept the men down there? Who's responsible for putting them there?
Spirit response: "Cave."
Ali: Cave Couts?
Ali: If it was Cave Couts, was it junior or senior?
Ali: Could you just, just clarify, junior or senior, please?
Spirit response: "Si."
Nicole: Thank you. Was it Cave Couts Sr. or Cave Couts Jr. that kept the men down there?
Spirit response: "Son."
Nicole: This is very emotional right now. You have to understand that for us, it's very hard, as we feel the sorrow and the pain that some of you may have suffered down there [in the root cellar]. We are so, so sorry. We are so, so sorry. Is there anything that we can do for you? I do want to repeat, and I know that some of you said you know; but for those that aren't sure, you have to trust me when I say this: you do not have to relive the terror, the anxiety, the pain and the torture of being down there anymore. You are free of that, and if you need help getting to the point where you do feel freedom, you need to let us know and we will help you.

It is extremely rare to acquire such profound and historically relevant responses from the spirit world. Had we not spent several years at the adobe building rapport with its spiritual residents, it is highly doubtful that we would have captured such chilling communication. The adobe's ethereal beings have come to trust us in our approach and somehow know that we conduct our work with respect, reverence and good intention. We are forever grateful for this communication session, as it has enabled us to learn more about the historical fabric of the adobe and it has further let the adobe's spirits know that we are there for them.

There are many paranormal experiences and evidence to suggest that Juan Gonzalez is one of the prevalent spirits at the adobe that communicates with Ali and me, as well as our tour guests. In fact, a man who addresses himself as "Juan" did not come through for the San Diego Paranormal Research Society until Ali joined the team and commenced her Spirits of the Adobe tour co-host gig. The very premiere night of Ali assisting the tours is when Juan introduced himself by his name. While our guests were situated in the majordomo room, Ali said, "You can use this

Looking north toward the backside of the L-shaped hacienda, where humanoid shadow figures have been spotted. *Courtesy of Ali Schreiber.*

device to tell us your name." Immediately following was a heavily accented male vocalization that came through saying "Juan," initiating a string of encounters with this particular ethereal entity. While all of us were responding to the above response, Nicole went ahead and said, "Wow, that was interesting." Shortly thereafter, a highly similar-sounding voice came through and said, "*Sí*." Since the time of this noteworthy experience, a man by the name of Juan continues to communicate to us almost every time we visit the Rancho Buena Vista Adobe.

Another poignant experience that lends to the possible fact that Juan Gonzalez may have Native American origins occurred on another tour night in 2016. Many paranormal researchers, such as myself, enjoy working intuitively or psychically by employing various empathic skills. While in the majordomo room, I suddenly felt the need to ask Juan if he was friends with the native peoples. Thus, I asked him, "Juan, were you friends with the Indians?" An immediate reply with a similar resonating vocalization occurred just moments later, answering, "Still am." Needless to say, all the people in our group were pleasantly surprised, with goose bumps popping out of their skin after hearing this salient response. This experience positively suggests that Juan knew the native population, further supporting the theory that he was adopted by the Coutses and used as an Indian servant until he reached the age of majority.

Another intriguing experience that sustains this postulation is evidenced in one of our encounters in the kitchen area that was added on by Ysidora Forster Fuller Couts Gray, one of the daughters of Cave J. Couts and Ysidora Bandini de Couts. We were conducting a divining rod session with our tour guests, as we have achieved promising results utilizing the rods in this adobe location. Typically, when addressing the rancho's spiritual residents, we designate the dowsing rods to cross like an "X" for "yes" answers and separate out into a "Y" shape for "no" answers. This method appears to work effectively. One night, we addressed Ysidora Bandini de Couts and asked her if Juan was close to her. Instantly, the rods crossed heavily. In addition, we had a few devices recording the session, and a faint "yes" can be heard answering my question. As a paranormal researcher, more pieces of the puzzle connect whenever you have two or more experiences that corroborate each other.

Apparition sightings are quite rare, and you must be gracious whenever you are blessed with visualizing one. Ghostly sightings are moderate at the Rancho Buena Vista Adobe and typically fall into the categories of shadow figure sightings and/or partially manifested ghost forms. Regardless, I recently had one of the most profound supernatural happenings in all my seven years of researching this most historic edifice. Our November 2017 tour was about to commence, so I walked out the entrance door to the guesthouse to look for any more guests making their way down the famed brick walkway off Alta Vista Drive. As I looked through the courtyard archway gate, I noticed two bare legs and the bottom half of a figure possibly adorned in a loincloth. Right away, my innate intuition told me that I was seeing Juan, as just moments before I had privately hoped that I would see Juan in spirit form. If this truly was a sighting of Juan Gonzalez, did he telepathically connect with me by granting my wish?

There are yet other interesting events concerning a spirit that goes by the name of Juan Gonzalez. The majordomo room where the said remains were discovered many years ago is not only a hot spot area for ghostly activity but also emanates a certain intelligent feel about it—it seems as though the space is alive with thought and emotion. Many people immediately report physical manifestations while entering this area, disclosing that they have headaches, chest tightness and/or weakness in the knees and lower extremities. Guests often claim to feel quite uneasy in this space, documenting dizziness or vertigo. It should be noted that no one has felt threatened or scared; rather, the sense that you are not alone is felt throughout the adobe, especially when standing in this particular room. Prior to knowing the uncanny history of the room, some individuals have sensed an eerie and anxious feeling adjacent to the wall enclosing the human skeletal remains. Juan seems to come through more often in the majordomo room—perhaps the most conspicuous aspect of it all.

We have had some further intriguing spirit communication with Juan. In early 2017, one of our friends was attending the Spirits of the Adobe tour when he had a fascinating encounter. While situated in the majordomo room, Ali proceeded to say, "Hello, this is Ali, Nicole, Eric and our friends Hope and Chuck; did somebody touch Chuck on the back of the head?" Eric then interjected, "Señor Gonzalez, do you know who touched Chuck's head?" A few seconds later, we heard a very clear male vocalization answer the questions by saying "Juan."

Furthermore, on another night conducting research, Ali asked, "Who was it that did most of the cooking at this rancho?" A female voice comes through expressing the name "Juan," which would make sense if he was utilized on the property as an indentured Indian servant. I then inquired about Juan's favorite food to cook, to which he responded "*frijoles*," or beans. In fact, Juan has been pretty forthcoming with us, sharing other intriguing pieces of information that directly coincide with the adobe's historical narrative.

Purposely saved toward the last, the most striking piece of spirit communication concerning Juan occurred in early 2016 while conducting our 9:30 p.m. tour. It is possible that the fictional character of Alessandro in Helen Hunt Jackson's novel *Ramona* is based on the real-life Juan Gonzalez. During our tour's master bedroom audio session in 2017, I proceeded to ask a very important question. I inquired, "Alessandro Asis also went by the name of whom? What was his name?" A female response occurred shortly after, saying "Juan Gonzalez." Furthermore, Ali asked Juan if he was present with the group, at which time we received an affirmative response. When asked if he was with anyone else, a male vocalization matching Juan's tone came through saying "Ysidora"—yet another link to Juan's relationship with the Couts matriarch as indentured servant.

While in the majordomo room during our 9:30 p.m. Spirits of the Adobe tour on December 15, 2017, our tour group was able to witness some very exciting results during one of our audio sessions with the spirit box. As mentioned, Juan Gonzalez has consistently talked with us on a monthly basis, at times letting us know that he's present with us and our tour attendees. This is exactly what occurred around 10:15 p.m. on this particular night, as he answered "yes" when Ali asked him if he was with us. I then proceeded to say, "Juan, it's always so nice to talk with you," at which time he said, "Thank you." A little bit later in our communication session, Ali asked Juan if he was friends with anyone in particular at the adobe. Intuitively, I thought of Sasaria and asked Juan if he knew her. A few moments later, we all heard an emphatic "yes," indicating that Juan knew of Sasaria. Just to ensure more confirmation, I then interjected, "Juan, did you and Sasaria live with Ysidora Bandini de Couts?" Again, another resounding "yes" was heard by all, thus corroborating the historical records of the Couts family raising native children.

Our most recent profound majordomo room encounter occurred during the 2017 holiday season. We inquired about the annual holiday that occurs in the month of December, asking the ethereal energies what it is called. I said, "The adobe is decorated so beautiful for the holiday that's approaching soon. It's Merry…" About two seconds later, a male vocalization was strongly heard saying "Christmas!" As if this session could not get more exciting, I also asked the spirits to tell us the name of the governor who deeded the original Rancho Buena Vista land to Felipe Subria in 1850. I proceeded to say, "Governor Pio…" and "Pico" clearly came through our communication device.

Now, during the time of the Rancho Buena Vista Adobe's heyday, there were many males named Juan; thus, it is possible that we may be interacting with more than one spirit by the same name. After doing extensive research at the Huntington Library, perusing through Cave Johnson Couts's journals, both Ali and I have considered some other possibilities. First, it may be possible that we are also conversing with a spirit by the name of Juan de la Cruz Bandini, a member of the celebrated family of Californians who passed away in a tragic accident while on his colt, which was hitched to a double-wheeled road cart. Brother to Ysidora Bandini de Couts, he was forty-eight years old at his untimely death. This catastrophe occurred on a road situated between the Vista and Altura ranchos. We have ruled out that the skeletal remains discovered in the adobe walls of the Rancho Buena Vista's majordomo room belonged to Juan de la Cruz Bandini, as his body was brought to Vista and embalmed. Furthermore, Cave Johnson Couts employed other Mexican workers by the name of Juan, as evidenced in his journals.

Another possibility concerns an individual by the name of Juan Mendoza, who was abruptly killed in Old Town by Cave J. Couts. A native of Chihuahua, Mexico, Mendoza resided about seven miles from Sausal Baja California as the alcalde of the San Antonio mines in 1858. After some ensuing difficulties and the murder of at least a dozen individuals, he became the majordomo to Mr. Couts. Apparently, the reason why he was employed by Couts had to do with his wife, Ysidora, who needed the services of Mendoza's wife. For about six to eight months prior to Mendoza's murder, Mr. Couts did not want to come to San Diego for fear of being killed by Juan Mendoza. It was Juan's assertion that Couts owed him money and that the former refused to pay. After Couts discharged Mendoza's employment, he consistently received death threats.

Once Couts decided to head to San Diego for business affairs, he brought a man with him in his buggy, presumably for extra security. His double-barrel gun was loaded with buckshot and placed across his lap. He stayed at the Colorado House in Old Town San Diego at night. The following morning, Couts stopped to talk with a Mr. Tibbetts at the small adobe house in the plaza; while there, he witnessed a man enter the Franklin House. After learning that it was his nemesis, Mendoza, he turned and faced the door. Mendoza soon came out of the building and walked toward Couts. As soon as Mendoza saw Couts's gun, he started to run toward his house. Couts called on Mendoza to stop, which he refused to do. Shots were then fired, which rapidly took Juan Mendoza's life. Cave J. Couts was found not guilty. Since Juan Mendoza knew Couts Sr., it is probably safe to assume that the two might continue their correspondence in spirit form as well. Since there was bad blood between the two in mortal form, perhaps these exact feelings have transferred over to their existence in the afterworld. Regardless of their perilous past, it is our hope that these men have found peace while in the heavens.

CHAPTER 4

THE LEGEND OF THE ADOBE'S LADY IN WHITE

The legend of the lady in white populates many haunted locations in California and beyond. The Southwest regions largely associate this female phantom with La Llorona, a distressed earthbound ghost who incessantly screams in agony by a water source after the death of her young children. Other famous sightings of this phantom white spirit have occurred at Old Town's El Fandango Restaurant, Escondido's Elfin Forest and the RMS *Queen Mary*. As for the Rancho Buena Vista Adobe, there is an entirely different theory for the origin of its ghostly female adorned in white clothing. When the San Diego Paranormal Research Society commenced both its Spirits of the Adobe tours and private research of the premises, we were told by adobe docents that the lady in white seen on the property is most likely the ethereal being of Ysidora Forster Fuller Couts Gray, one of the daughters of Cave J. Couts and Ysidora Bandini de Couts.

There is a historical reason why many people believe that this ghost is the spirit form of this particular Couts daughter. Remember that the younger Ysidora lost the property to foreclosure, which caused her to deal with depression and sadness. However, the elder Ysidora, the matriarch of the family, might choose to remain at the rancho as a way to oversee its use in modern times. Based on seven-plus years of intensive historical and paranormal research of the property, both Ali Schreiber and I strongly believe that this feminine phantom may be Ysidora Bandini de Couts. Perhaps there are two lady in white spirits, both mother and daughter.

View of the Rancho Buena Vista Adobe's courtyard from the verandas, circa 1957–73. *Courtesy of Vista Historical Society.*

At the beginning of our haunted history tours, we bring our guests through the iconic arched ivy-laced gate, which proudly opens into the luscious courtyard. Once inside this ornate quad, we talk about the huge magnolia tree that was said to be a gift to the Pollards by legendary actress Joan Crawford. We then segue into discussion about one of the most popular supernatural claims associated with the Rancho Buena Vista: the famed lady in white. After sharing the possible theories of her genesis, we share some of the documented sightings of her along the outside veranda, as well as inside the various rooms.

Spanning the course of many years, many employees and visitors to the adobe have witnessed this particular specter roaming inside the courtyard. Most people have described a shorter woman with dark hair adorned in some sort of white dress or gown elegantly walking and/or gliding along the L-shaped structure's veranda that was installed by Cave J. Couts when he owned the property. It's unknown at this time whether this female entity possesses any spiritual intelligence versus being residual in origin (a psychic imprint from long ago that is sensed in modern times). Chances are that both ghostly mom and daughter have some sort of ethereal intellect, as our many otherworldly encounters with both of them allude to, which will be elaborated on in the paragraphs to come.

Left: This large magnolia tree was gifted to the Pollards by legendary actress Joan Crawford. *Courtesy of Ali Schreiber*.

Below: A portion of the Rancho Buena Vista Adobe's courtyard, where numerous weddings take place each year. *Courtesy of Vista Historical Society*.

City of Vista staff enter the Rancho Buena Vista in the early morning hours to set up for daily events or to take care of gardening. In fact, during the dawn hours, two employees witnessed a woman adorned in white come up to them as they were working in the adobe's courtyard. Apparently, the female asked these men if they needed any assistance. When they started to answer her, they noticed that she had completely vanished. There was absolutely no way a living person could have disappeared in that quick of a time. Of course, this experience left the men stupefied; it has been said that one of these workers quit his job after the encounter.

During our tenure at the Rancho Buena Vista Adobe, the sala has been a premium spot for lady in white encounters, especially through the glass door that gives a partial glimpse into the courtyard. During our December 15, 2017 7:00 p.m. tour, one of our guests commented that he saw a translucent figure wearing white clothing dart from a left to right position. When asked about physical characteristics, this individual said that the encounter happened so fast that he couldn't make out any specifics, which is quite common with apparitional sightings.

My mom, Norma Strickland, has been a frequent guest on our haunted history tours. About three years ago, while the group was situated in the sala during a spirit communication session, my mom may have witnessed the lady in white. In her own words, this is what she had to say in regard to this encounter:

> When you are on the tour and you go through the dining room, through the kitchen and then outside, I can't say that I saw anything, but I felt something, and it was cold. As you proceed through the tour and into the great room [sala], I saw something else. Through the glass door in between the piano and red fringed lamp, I saw something white—possibly the lady in white.

Perhaps the lady in white feels a fondness for my mom, as she has had other occurrences with this female entity. Again, in her own words, she shares these profound encounters:

> There are a few experiences. One occurred when I sat down to read a book in the guesthouse sitting room where you show the video to tour guests. I was reading my book, and there was no one around, and through my peripheral vision, I saw something go by outside of the glass French doors. It looked like a younger female in a light-color dress with darker hair. So I made sure

A modern view of the sala depicting the central focal point: the chandelier. The piano has played of its own volition, in addition to a female apparition playing the organ. *Author's collection.*

I got up and looked outside to make sure no one was outside, and there was nothing there. But I know what I saw, and I got goose bumps.

Another intriguing occurrence possibly indicating the lady in white's presence inside the adobe occurred during a private research project in the children's room. Both Ali and I were preparing to commence an EVP session. We sat down comfortably on the floor and started our vigil—a quiet time reserved for gleaning the impressions of the environment. After about ten minutes, we started our line of questioning, mainly making inquiries into the history of the adobe. About halfway through, we heard the disembodied sounds of someone walking around in a dress. There was definitely a *swish swish* noise of fabric touching fabric, very similar to what it would sound like if a person walked around while adorned in a thick, flowing dress. These resonances only lasted a couple of seconds and vanished as quickly as they appeared. We ruled out the possibility of the sounds generating from the outside, since we were the only two individuals inside the structure at this time, so we really do not have a logical explanation for this eerie occurrence.

A modern-day view of the beautiful dining room with a bay window looking out onto the courtyard. *Author's collection.*

There are two doorways in the sala that lead to other portions of the L-shaped adobe structure: one that leads from the sala to the makeshift chapel and another that leads from the sala to the master bedroom. Both of these doorways are hot spots in that apparitional sightings have been documented in both of them. Typically, during the tour group's collective audio session, I sit on the steps adjacent to the ornate little chapel, mainly to have a good view of the entire crowd. There have been a few occurrences when guests have noticed a possible ghostly form standing or hovering behind me. When asked to describe the characteristics of this specter, witnesses have disclosed it being white, translucent and possibly wearing a dress. Others have also described it as a grayish humanoid shadow form.

On a recent tour in the winter months of 2017, Ali and I had back-to-back encounters, not knowing the other's experience until after it occurred, thus ruling out the power of suggestion. In the darkness, while situated in front of the great room's vintage grand piano, a flowing spirit form adorned in very light clothing glided right past me. With a matching description, Ali openly shared how she saw a ghostly form proceed into the sala and move in my direction. Both of us experienced this moving specter as it made its way across the great room before vanishing into thin air.

The lady in white makes herself known throughout the Rancho Buena Vista Adobe. There is a particular spot in the great room that provides visual access to other rooms in the L-shaped structure. On many occasions, whether they are on tour nights or private research evenings, we have documented physical movement at both ends of the structure when there aren't any living people in those locations. Furthermore, there have been instances when we have seen ghostly forms moving about while looking through the doorways that connect all the rooms.

Another possible sighting of the lady in white occurred one night while we were situated in the sala. Among the silence, we heard odd sounds emanating from either the bathroom or the gathering room. Remember that these rooms are on the north side of the sala. There was a variety of noises that sounded as if someone was just going about their business. All in all, they lasted a few seconds. Shortly after, one of our tour guests announced that she saw a white ghostly form move in the exact same space where the sounds originated. Any anomalous activity leans more toward being paranormal in origin whenever you can have two personal experiences corroborate each other.

Disembodied male vocalizations have emanated from this room, which lies adjacent to the majordomo room. Maria Antonia's children apparently slept in this space when she owned the adobe. *Author's collection.*

Although not adorned in the classic white dress or gown, there is another spotted female apparition who is seen inside the hacienda from time to time. This particular entity is often witnessed wearing an emerald-green vintage dress. She has also been seen near the gathering room from the sala's vantage point. To date, we don't know who she is; however, there has been some ethereal response to the name "Elizabeth." Applying critical thinking, could this particular spirit actually be the lady in white fully manifested in spirit form, which allows viewers to completely make out her attire's color? If it is the same entity, perhaps she shows up as a vague white form when only partially manifested. Maybe she hails from the time when the Pollards lived at the rancho. The Pollards were known to invite Hollywood's elite to lavish parties at the rancho during their tenure. Along the lines of this theory, maybe this lady in green is a residual sighting from the 1930s to the 1950s.

CHAPTER 5

THE COUTS FAMILY'S ETHEREAL REIGN

The Rancho Buena Vista Adobe has been hospitable to some famous proprietors and/or residents over its years. One of these individuals was Colonel Cave Johnson Couts, also known as Don Cuevas, who hailed from Springfield, Tennessee. One of the main people intertwined in the historical tapestry of San Diego, Couts can be found in almost any Southern California history book. Born in 1821, Cave graduated from West Point in 1843 and became the second lieutenant of the Second Dragoons on July 1, 1843. During the war of 1848 between Mexico and the United States, he served on frontier duty. He then became attached to the First Dragoons, who were mandated to march on to California. It was in May 1848 that the elder Couts was ordered to San Diego to operate a military escort for the United States Mexican boundary commissioners.

It was during this time that Cave met the love of his life during his tenure as a house guest of Juan Lorenzo Bandini, another renowned figure in San Diego's history. Bandini was a noted prominent official under the Mexican government. Significantly educated, he was one of the first San Diego residents to form an alliance with the Americans during the war with Mexico. Couts was introduced to and had intimate relations with Ysidora Bandini, Juan's youngest daughter. She was revered by many and thought to be the most beautiful woman in all of Southern California. She was known for her optimism, loving nature and professional demeanor.

On April 5, 1851, Cave wed Ysidora at the Casa Bandini in San Diego. As a wedding gift, Abel Stearns, Ysidora's brother-in-law, gave the 2,219-acre

Rancho Guajome to the blissful couple. This was also the year that Cave quit his affairs with the army in October. Once commissioned as colonel, Couts became quite active with the San Diego community. He was credited with reorganizing the county government, arranging the first school district and serving on the county's premiere grand jury and a term as county judge. He was also an Indian sub-agent at Mission San Luis Rey, possibly helping to explain the elusive legend of Juan Gonzalez, which you have already read about.

Cave J. Couts in military attire. "Detail." *The Huntington Library, Cave J. Couts Journals. Courtesy of the Huntington Library, San Marino, California.*

When reading about Colonel Couts's reign at Rancho Guajome, we can certainly agree that he was destined to live the rancho lifestyle. In 1852, he heavily concentrated on designing and building Vista's Rancho Guajome. Constructed around an eighty-by ninety-foot courtyard with a focal point fountain, the lavish edifice was entirely self-contained. To help with financial matters, he made several cattle herd drives and gold field expeditions to Northern California. During this period, Couts became quite the real estate investor, having first purchased the Rancho Buena Vista. He then bought the Rancho Vallecitos de San Marcos and Rancho La Jolla, collectively equaling an excess of twenty thousand acres. If that wasn't enough, it is thought that the resourceful Couts also planted San Diego's premiere orange grove and irrigation system.

Harrison and Ruth Doyle, in their book *A History of Vista*, go on to say, "By this time Guajome had become practically self-sustaining—a live community in itself. There was a small store, a carpenter shop, a smithy, a harness and saddler's shop and a bakery. There were quarters for farm hands, servants and vaqueros, together with a school and teacher, teamsters and guards."

An excerpt from Elliot's *History of San Diego and San Bernardino Counties* describes Cave Johnson as a

> *tall, commanding figure a little over six feet in height, weighing about 165 pounds, straight as an arrow, willowy and active, a perfect horseman, the beau ideal of a cavalry officer, with natural instincts of a gentleman*

supplemented by a thorough education; fond of an active, busy life, devoted to his family, the soul of honor; to him a lie was like blasphemy, being inexcusable and unpardonable; of strict integrity and business habits, he was also jovial, and a genial companion, fond of jokes, music and dancing, a thorough man of business and a perfect gentleman in society.

After reading Elliot's quote about Cave Johnson Couts, it is hard to believe that he was also known to be quite harsh, especially to the native peoples. In 1855, the grand jury twice accused him of abusing Indians with a riata. Cave was acquitted on one of these counts and dismissed on a technicality for the other. When squatters arrived and infiltrated the ranchos after the decline of smallpox and the great drought, Couts and his brother were charged with murdering five unlawful tenants—four Indians and one African American—in 1865. The case was later dismissed. Yet again, in 1866, Couts was indicted for the killing of Juan Mendoza, which was previously discussed. In my personal opinion, I believe that Cave Johnson Couts was a decent man who, at times, fell victim to not only stress but also the way society behaved during those days. In other words, it was one man for himself during his era; in order to survive, one had to be tough and resourceful. Even the Indians he managed both loved and feared him, suggesting that he had a caring heart despite his tough exterior. Couts passed away in San Diego on June 10, 1874. Ysidora Bandini de Couts continued to live at the Rancho Guajome and managed it until her death in 1897.

Mr. and Mrs. Cave Johnson Couts had ten children, with eight of those living to adulthood. Some of these Couts offspring have also made ethereal appearances at the Rancho Buena Vista, including Maria Antonia, Cave Couts Jr., Ysidora Fuller Couts Gray, William and Robert Lee Couts. Following is a small summary of each child.

Abel Stearns Couts: Born in San Diego on January 21, 1852; passed away at Rancho Guajome on October 27, 1855.

Maria Antonia Arcadia Couts: Born in San Diego on June 13, 1853; passed away in Los Angeles on September 10, 1936.

Guillermo (William) Antonio Couts: Born at Rancho Guajome on December 7, 1854; passed away in Los Angeles in 1935.

Cave Johnson Couts Jr.: Born at Rancho Guajome on June 5, 1856; passed away at the same location on July 22, 1943.

Ana Venancia Couts: Born at Rancho Guajome on November 25, 1857; passed away in Los Angeles on December 15, 1868.

Couts family photograph. "Detail." *The Huntington Library, Cave J. Couts Journals. Courtesy of the Huntington Library, San Marino, California.*

Ysidora Forster Couts: Born at Rancho Guajome on October 23, 1860; passed away in Los Angeles in 1952.

Elena Francisca Couts: Born at Rancho Guajome on August 18, 1862; date of death unknown.

Robert (Roberto) Lee Couts: Born at Rancho Guajome on April 17, 1864; passed away in Los Angeles on November 18, 1920.

John Forster Couts: Born at Rancho Guajome on May 20, 1866; date of death unknown.

Maria Carolina Couts: Born at Rancho Guajome on February 28, 1868; passed away in Los Angeles on December 1, 1944.

We have made a couple of visits to the Huntington Library in San Marino, California, as it houses an extensive archive of Cave Johnson Couts diaries, journals and letters. Along with papers from Cave Couts Jr., this collection makes up approximately sixteen thousand pieces. While going through these priceless historical documents, you can viscerally feel what life was like for Cave J. Couts and his family during the rancho era. What is most unanticipated is the fact that we've been able to verify portions of history by comparing certain paranormal evidence to actual historical information. This is what genuine supernatural research is all about—being able to examine portions of ghostly encounters to see where they fit on the historical time continuum.

Authentic evidence suggests that both Cave Johnson Couts and his wife, Ysidora Bandini de Couts, are spiritually residing at the Rancho Buena Vista Adobe in modern times. In addition to proprietorship of this rancho and the Rancho Vallecitos de San Marcos, they also owned and lived at the nearby Rancho Guajome. Since they never stayed at the Rancho Buena Vista, it makes their reason for appearing there in spirit form even more elusive. There are many possibilities for this: 1) As you will read in later chapters, some of Cave and Ysidora's children resided on the property; 2) Even though they never inhabited the hacienda, they must have felt great pride in ownership; 3) In ethereal form, perhaps Cave and Ysidora, as well as some of their children, feel it necessary to look after the structure in modern times.

For the past seven-plus years, the San Diego Paranormal Research Society has had intriguing encounters with the patriarch and matriarch of this legendary San Diego pioneer family, as well as some of their children. Again, the couple never lived at the Rancho Buena Vista Adobe, but it seems that their energy is ever-present throughout the property. As mentioned, it's as if they are spiritually looking after the property they once owned. Intriguingly, when we first commenced our Spirits of the Adobe tours, one of our guest psychic mediums immediately connected with a spiritual entity matching Cave Couts's physical attributes and demeanor. Intuitively speaking, this guest strongly sensed a male spirit following the group around from room to room, almost as if he was monitoring the tour's events. Additionally, the medium also picked up on some other male otherworldly energies that wouldn't come into certain rooms when Cave's spirit was present. If the psychic was correct on his senses, could this be indicative of servants and/or native people's intimidation of Cave when he owned the rancho?

Perhaps the psychic medium was picking up on Cave Johnson Couts Jr., who did stay at the Rancho Buena Vista to look after his prized horses. In the 1930s, the younger Cave mentioned to a *Southern California Rancher* editor that he owned one of the finest saddle horses in San Diego County. One night while at the Rancho Buena Vista to ensure the safety of the property due to roaming bandits, Cave Couts Jr. housed his beloved stallion in one of the bedrooms. As the night progressed, a man came to the property, introduced himself as the deputy sheriff and asked to stay the night. Cave gave him dinner and a comfortable bed. The two stayed up into the early morning hours discussing the concept of Southern California bandits, especially one man by the name of Julian Chavez. The younger Couts must have felt relatively safe, as he showed his renowned horse to this alleged law enforcer. When sunrise came, the two men ate a substantial breakfast. As the guest was leaving the property, he revealed his true identity to Couts, saying that he was the real Julian Chavez. He confessed that he came to the Rancho Buena Vista to steal the stallion but changed his mind after experiencing Couts's kindness and hospitality.

Maybe father and son both make appearances at the adobe from time to time. We tend to ask many historically related questions to the spirits during our paranormal research projects. We try not to make our sessions sound interrogative or like an interview; rather, we tend to keep them more along the lines of two-way communication sessions. When asking about the history of the Rancho Buena Vista Adobe, we've heard many different male and spirit female voices answer with "Cave" or "Couts." Of course, these answers can indicate father or son or both; it's hard to tell.

As mentioned, over the years, we have been able to document and collect various paranormal audio segments pertaining to the spirits of the Couts immediate family members. The following are some of our most captivating and unique communication captures.

Cave Couts Jr. "Detail." *The Huntington Library, Cave J. Couts Journals. Courtesy of the Huntington Library, San Marino, California.*

During one of our experiments, Nicole asked the ethereal energies, "What family do you work for?" About two seconds after, a female spirit came through saying, "Cave." She most likely was referring to the elder Cave Couts, as he was the proprietor of the Rancho Buena Vista Adobe. Additionally, Nicole then proposed, "Who owns the adobe right now?" A disembodied female whisper of "Couts" was heard immediately after.

During a tour night, one of our guests intuitively sensed the presence of an ethereal being. So she asked, "Were you standing next to me, trying to tell me something?" Then, all of a sudden, we heard phantom movement emanating from the sala area. I then asked, "Is there someone in the sala? Can you say yes or no?" About six to seven seconds quietly went by, and all of a sudden, a deep-throated male vocalization came through emphatically saying, "Cave." It was extremely loud and clear, so I confirmed, "Cave; you all heard that, right?" Ali then inquired, "Is Cave Sr. or Cave Jr. with us?" After a short period, Ali announced that she heard the disembodied voice of a woman answer "Cave Sr."

In late 2016, while we were conducting paranormal experiments in the adobe's master bedroom, we were unaware of the striking spirit communication encounter about to be unleashed. There are historical images of young Cave Johnson Couts in military uniform, as well as photos of his daughter Maria Antonia and her husband, Chalmers Scott, hanging up on the room's walls. Additionally, an army jacket lies on a stool at the base of the bed, an artifact that may spur on spiritual activity from time to time. During this time, we specifically addressed questions to Cave Johnson Couts about his military career. At the beginning of our session, we heard a disembodied male vocalization echo the word "hello" through our real-time communication device. Ali then asked, "Whoever said 'hello,' can you tell us your name again please?" About five quiet seconds passed before hearing a phantom answer of "Couts."

Ali started out the second line of questioning by saying, "Mr. Couts, if you are with us, I see a picture of you here on the wall of you wearing a uniform. What branch of the military did you serve in?" Immediately after her inquiry, a phantom male voice uttered the word "captain" through our spirit box, which correlates to the known fact that Couts was a colonel in the army. I then thanked Cave for his participation, and immediately after, the word "sergeant" was said.

When we've captured striking evidence during a discussion about specific history relating to Cave Johnson Couts Sr., then it's safe to assume that particular piece of evidence concerns father, not son. For example, Cave Johnson Couts Sr. is most likely being referenced when we've received a spirit response of "Cave" to the question, "Who owned the Rancho Buena Vista Adobe?" We know this because the elder male Couts member originally purchased and subsequently owned the entire property. When we've captured interesting responses to the noted stallion that stayed inside the hacienda at night, then it's safe to assume those replies alluded to Cave Johnson Couts Jr.

In addition to father and son having the same name, both of them take after each other in looks, demeanor and personality. Cave Couts Jr. continued his dad's legacy by being hospitable to many notable individuals, such as President Grant and Helen Hunt Jackson. Intriguingly, on our private paranormal investigations of the adobe as well as our Spirits of the Adobe tours, we have heard two different disembodied vocalizations say "Cave" and "Couts" during spirit communication sessions addressing the Couts family. They sound similar; however, one voice is a bit deeper than the other, and we feel this to be the ethereal vocalization of Cave Couts Jr. We've come to this strong possibility after several sessions while addressing the prized stallion on the Rancho Buena Vista property. Being that this horse belonged to Cave Couts Jr., it's only logical to assume that he would answer questions in spirit form about his animal. This is most likely what occurred one night during our Spirits of the Adobe tours.

During our 9:30 p.m. tour, we asked Cave Couts Jr. a couple of interesting questions about his horses. I asked, "How many horses do you have?" A deep-throated male vocalization occurred through our spirit box device clearly and profoundly answering "three." We then inquired about the animals' colors and received that identical-sounding male voice, which said "appy," possibly indicating "appaloosa." Ali has owned horses all of her life, so her instincts kicked in as she asked, "Do you have any appaloosa horses?" Almost immediately after, this indistinguishable vocalization came through emphatically answering "two." This is an example of the many clear, profound and historically relevant audio captures we've collected over the years at the Rancho Buena Vista Adobe.

A similar situation exists between both Ysidora Bandini de Couts and Ysidora Couts Gray, mother and daughter, respectively. Over the years during our paranormal research at the Rancho Buena Vista Adobe, we've captured a lot of spirit audio pertaining to both women. With spirit answers of "Ysidora," it is quite difficult to fathom whether it's a reference to mother or daughter. However, different nicknames for both women have helped clear up the confusion. The elder Ysidora went by the nickname of "Dona," whereas her daughter went by "Izzy." Believe it or not, we've recorded ethereal vocalizations indicating one or the other from time to time. Furthermore, we've come to recognize Ysidora Bandini de Couts's spiritual voice. It typically comes through breathy and whispery. The younger Ysidora has a higher vocal tone; considering this, it's easier to decipher which Ysidora is communicating to us at any given moment.

In fact, the elder Mrs. Couts told us her nickname one night on December 16, 2016, while the group was situated in the master bedroom. I inquired, "Ysidora Bandini de Couts, you also went by a different name. Or people called you by a different name as well. Can you share that with us?" Our spirit box device momentarily stopped scanning, which it is not programmed to do of its own volition. Ali then said, "Ysidora, I'm sorry. My device stopped. Can you answer Nicole's question please?" Matching the breathy vocalization of the Couts matriarch, a female voice came through saying, "Dona" almost immediately after. This is one of those convincing examples that strongly suggested we were hearing from Ysidora Bandini de Couts as opposed to her daughter.

Sadly, we know that Ysidora Couts Gray lost the Rancho Buena Vista Adobe to financial foreclosure. There is even a forlorn photo depicting her with her hand covering her face as she sat in a carriage. When you glance at this particular picture, you can immediately sense the loss and pain associated with losing the beloved hacienda. It is for this reason that many feel the meandering lady in white is Couts Gray's ghostly form. Mothers have a tight bond with their daughters, and this union profoundly survives death. Ysidora Bandini de Couts very well could be looking after her daughter, especially if she is still dealing with the loss of her home in spirit. Perhaps the elder Couts made a deal with her husband and promised him that she would always look after the ranchos he owned, even in death. Then again, there may be reasons we mortals are not permitted to know why spiritual energies choose to exist at certain locales.

In my opinion, a paranormal researcher has hit gold when there is an intuitive impression of a particular ghost or spirit followed by captured evidence matching that psychic sense. This has occurred many times at the Rancho Buena Vista Adobe. During one of our spirit communication sessions in the majordomo room, Nicole started to get the strong sense that Ysidora Bandini de Couts had walked into the room to join the guests. Thus, she asked, "Ysidora, are you present with us?" A breathy female vocalization matching Ysidora's came through answering "*Sí.*" The excited expressions on people's faces were indeed priceless. Ali then asked, "Are you wearing your pretty dress?" Couts answered by saying, "Yes." This encounter goes to show that some ghosts and spirits may choose to speak in more than one language. We have had many instances at the hacienda where a particular entity will speak in English and then Spanish or vice versa.

Another uncanny event took place on June 19, 2015, while in the majordomo room during one of our Spirits of the Adobe tours. I inquired, "Are we speaking to Juan or Luis or both?" About twenty-seven seconds later, a response emanated through our device answering "Juan." The elder Ysidora was also asked if she was present with the group, to which she replied, "*Sí.*" We believe that Mrs. Couts appears in spirit form quite often but doesn't always overtly communicate. However, there are those golden moments when all of a sudden, her distinct vocalization will come through.

Maria Antonia has spiritually communicated with us as well via her breathy whispered voice. Her vocal tone is a bit different than her mother's. While interviewing Frank Rojano on some of his otherworldly experiences at the rancho, he went on to share, in his own words, one of the first paranormal encounters ever documented at the property during the early 1990s. Quite possibly, Maria Antonia's spirit was the ethereal star of this occurrence:

This didn't happen to me; it happened to a florist. It was a hint, I guess, of the types of experiences that can occur here. We didn't have a museum yet, as we were still renting our rooms from the house because it wasn't completely furnished yet. We were in the process of acquiring all of the antiques and furniture.

They rented out the sala, and the group that rented it hired a florist to decorate for a party. He was arranging flowers everywhere, and my job was to open up the building for him, let him in and when he was done, go back and close it. A couple of hours later, he calls me up saying that he's ready to leave, as he can't stand this old lady here anymore. I asked him, "What old lady? What does she look like?" He said that she was wearing period dress, like an 1800s type of dress.

The following day, he was here taking out all of the flower arrangements, easels, vases and stuff he had. So, I showed the florist a picture [of Maria Antonia], the one that's in the master bedroom over the dresser, and he confirmed that the lady he saw looked a lot like her. He went on to say, "Gosh, that was her, I am pretty sure." He couldn't positively identify her, but it looked a lot like the woman in the photo. I didn't tell him that maybe he encountered one of the ghosts, as I didn't want to scare him.

The florist thought that she was a docent, too, so she must have looked quite real—not like a ghost but a real person. She was complaining as to where he was putting the flowers, so that is why he got upset. Anything he did, she complained.

So, he leaves, and I go in there to close it all up. I am looking all around for the lady, as I don't want to lock her in. I go to the end of the building, and I didn't see anyone. I looked all around, and no one was there, so I ended up closing up the place.

At first, I thought it might have been one of the docents, but the funny thing is that we didn't have any yet. Then I thought it was Claire, who was running the adobe back in those days. So I called Claire and asked her if she was at the adobe, and she said, "No, I am at home," as she lived in San Diego back then. I told her what was going on, and she confirmed that they had not hired any docents yet.

Now, remember that Maria's mother gifted the Rancho Buena Vista Adobe to her and her husband, Chalmers Scott, as a wedding present. Since she resided at the property for some time, it would make complete sense that she was quite particular about the items and decorations in her home. The florist's contact with Maria Antonia's spirit does highly corroborate our ethereal documentation with her some twenty-plus years later.

It is quite possible that the spirits of William Couts and his brother Robert Lee Couts commune with the living. Even though these two men passed away in later adulthood, we do have experiences and evidence combined that suggest they make ethereal appearances as children. Many paranormal researchers hypothesize that some ghosts and spirits choose to interact with the mortal world in child form possibly because their childhood was the most enjoyable. Perhaps it's plausible that these two Couts brothers manifest as both adult and youthful energies. Either way, we have had some intriguing otherworldly encounters with them.

In 2015, while co-hosting the Spirits of the Adobe tours in the sala, we experimented by asking some questions to William and Robert Lee. Ali

The vanity display in the master bedroom, where historical photographs of Maria Antonia and Chalmers Scott adorn the walls. *Author's collection.*

The north-facing view of the Rancho Buena Vista Adobe's courtyard. *Courtesy of Vista Historical Society.*

proceeded by asking, "William or Robert, are either one of you here?" As you may have already guessed, a male child's disembodied voice occurred a few seconds later saying "me." As the spirit communication session ensued, I excitedly said, "Hi, William." A few seconds later, we all heard a phantom little boy's voice loudly echo the word "hi" in return. All of us were quite surprised and had smiles running from ear to ear.

It seems as though some of the rancho's beloved ethereal energies have become quite familiar with our tour routine. For the past couple of years, Mrs. Couts, almost like clockwork, knows when we drive up Alta Vista Drive about 6:15 p.m. on the third Friday of each month. As we grab our equipment bags and lock up our vehicles, we proceed down the lined brick pathway to the adobe's paradise. As we inch closer, we see a familiar spiritual figure standing in front of the arched courtyard gate, almost as if she is greeting us. It must be her way of welcoming us back to the Rancho Buena Vista Adobe. Whether she appears to all guests is unknown; however, it's a strong inclination that she has come to not only understand our routine but also acknowledge her acceptance in what we do for the adobe's tours.

CHAPTER 6

HOLLYWOOD VISITS THE RANCHO BUENA VISTA ADOBE

Hollywood came to the Rancho Buena Vista Adobe in 1931 with new residents Harry Pollard and his wife, Margarita Fischer, a legendary silent-screen actress. Pollard was also an American silent-film actor and made his mark in the industry as a powerful director. Having commenced his career on the stage, Harry joined the Selig Polyscope Company in 1912 and subsequently acted in many of its movies. The Pollards were credited with substantially renovating the site, putting forth a pretty penny to accomplish the task. When Harry passed away in 1934, Margarita continued her individual sojourn at the property for many years.

For the first three decades of the twentieth century, Margarita's fame as a dominating stage and silent screen actress skyrocketed. According to Theresa St. Romain's book *Margarita Fischer: A Biography of the Silent Film Star*, the legendary actress changed her public image in order to remain appealing as she progressed from her teenage years to being a bona fide star. During her teenage years, she headed her own theatrical company. She entered film in 1910 and, just four short years after, led the American Film Manufacturing Company's Beauty variety of films. Hollywood stardom comes at a cost, and Margarita was no exception. St. Romain further stipulates, "She made both risky, innovative pictures and formulaic romantic comedies, although the former strained her marriage to the intensely private director Harry Pollard, and the latter frustrated her artistically."

She began touring at the tender age of twelve and was coerced into retiring from the screen in 1921 as a means of looking after her steadily alcoholic husband and preserving her precarious marriage. When the couple's personal affairs as well as Harry's career became more stable, Margarita returned to film acting, completing three more projects by the mid-1920s. Having difficulty recapturing her former celebrity prominence, Margarita retired yet again for the final time at Harry's request after her stint as a leading actress in *Uncle Tom's Cabin*.

She became Harry's ultimate support as he created substantial works for MGM prior to becoming ill in 1934. After quitting film work, Margarita briefly returned to the local stage for a while before living the remainder of her days quietly. Her three pastimes included traveling, tending to her family and becoming visibly active in local humanitarian work.

Legendary silent-screen actress Margarita Fischer Pollard, who owned the Rancho Buena Vista from 1931 to 1951 along with her husband, Harry Pollard. *Courtesy of Vista Historical Society.*

As with so many other silent-film moguls, Margarita's persona and body of works have largely been forgotten. However, in her later years, she acquired an intrigue in her acting legacy. Prior to her passing in 1975, she endeavored to protect her cinematic marvels via correspondence, interviews and other types of publicity. Regardless of her pragmatic efforts, Margarita's Hollywood resume remains buried and silent in modern times due to a lack of film preservation and altering preferences among the masses.

It's hard to know whether the Pollards are at the adobe in spirit form, as we've not captured distinguishable evidence of them. With this said, we have documented some intriguing experiences that possibly suggest the presence of these Hollywood moguls at the rancho. During one of our early Spirits of the Adobe tours, the group was asking questions to both Harry and Margarita; at one point, I asked if they were present with us. Immediately after my question, a definitive "Hi" emanated through one of our audio devices. Subsequently, I said, "Wow, it's great to be speaking to two great Hollywood stars," at which time the words "thank you" clearly followed. During the same communication session, I proposed for the spirit(s) to tell

The renowned bathroom that the Pollards renovated, circa 1957–73. The vanity's white stool once moved of its own volition during a Spirits of the Adobe tour. *Courtesy of Vista Historical Society.*

us their names. A few moments after, the name "Harry" flowed through the device, possibly indicating Harry Pollard. Needless to say, everyone's eyes were wide open with surprise.

On both private research projects and Spirits of the Adobe tours, we have asked comparative questions, as it is theorized that it may be easier for an ethereal entity to answer in this fashion. We also ask specific questions that allude to the specific time when the Pollards owned the adobe. One of our most popular inquiries entails preferred types of liquor. So, on one occasion, we captured a disembodied vocalization saying "whiskey" to our question of "Do you prefer vodka or whiskey?" Now, this particular type of alcohol was popular during the 1800s as well, so it's hard to completely discern who answered. However, the Pollards entertained many Hollywood elites during their tenure at the Rancho Buena Vista Adobe, and we all know that sophisticated alcoholic drinks were to be had.

The Pollards threw lavish parties for their equally famous guests in the sala grande. Just imagine Hollywood's elite coming together in affluent dress and dancing the night away to popular music. On another occasion, we inquired about a favorite type of routine among celebrities of that era. Interestingly, we received a ghostly reply of what sounded like "the waltz." There have been many sightings of floating ethereal energies gliding about the sala on many occasions. Applying some creativity, we have wondered if these occurrences are residual depictions of dancing spirits. Theory holds that places tend to trap various emotions, almost like a psychic imprint on the properties. Since happiness and euphoria are two emotions linked with parties and get-togethers, it goes to show that there may be residual paranormal events playing over and over like a record player at the adobe.

Another intriguing experience occurred one night on a Spirits of the Adobe tour. The time frame of the following question is enough to suggest the Pollards' era, as this particular actress was becoming quite popular during the 1950s. For creative purposes as well as a love for this particular Hollywood queen, we proposed, "Did Lucille Ball and Desi Arnaz ever visit the Rancho Buena Vista Adobe during one of your parties?" A very faint but discernible female spirit vocalization came through answering "yes." Did Margarita answer this question, or was it the Queen of Comedy herself who politely responded? We are still in the process of verifying this aforementioned piece of evidence to see if it's indeed a fact that the *I Love Lucy* stars visited the hacienda.

We have captured some incredibly profound spirit vocalizations at the Rancho Buena Vista Adobe. We have documented male and female vocalizations identifying themselves with the first and last names of previous adobe proprietors. As with other owners, the name "Margarita" has come through one of our gadgets designed for real-time communication with the departed. Forensic voice analysis will help us to better determine whether Margarita Fischer has, in fact, talked to us in ghostly form. We can compare our captures with actual real audio of the star to see if there's an inherent match.

In my humble opinion, I don't feel that the Pollards are permanent spiritual residents of the Rancho Buena Vista Adobe. Nevertheless, it seems as though they may ethereally visit their former home from time to time. Artifacts from their period still remain in the home, especially in the bathroom, which may serve as a trigger for them to manifest spiritually. Indeed, the Pollards contributed to this iconic Vista landmark in so many ways, and there's always a palpable reminder of the couple there in modern times.

CHAPTER 7
ANIMAL SPIRITS ROAMING THE PROPERTY

CAVE COUTS JR.'S PHANTOM STALLION

We know that a vast array of cattle and other animals were vital to the overall success of the rancho system. The proprietors of these vast land grants prided themselves on the raising of cattle and sheep. Substantial herds of these types of grazing animals helped provide hides for New England show manufacturers, as well as tallow-made soap for South America. Additionally, they provided beef for the influx of fortune seekers during the California gold rush. Furthermore, rancho owners and/or residents had esteemed horses on the property and went to great lengths to protect them from horse bandits and outlaws. When Cave Johnson Couts purchased the Rancho Buena Vista Adobe, he intended to raise cattle and livestock on the premises. In fact, his cattle herd increased by thousands.

It didn't initially become apparent to the San Diego Paranormal Research Society that the Rancho Buena Vista Adobe's paranormal tapestry included animal ghosts and spirits. It was only after conducting several Spirits of the Adobe tours and private research projects on the property that we became fully aware of these reports. Throughout recent years, we have individually documented, as well as from our tour guests, several encounters with ethereal animal beings on the premises.

The Rancho Buena Vista Adobe's most popular animal specter is Cave Couts Jr.'s revered stallion that was kept in the original adobe room at night, as many thieves were specifically after this steed. This small space was appropriately labeled the "stinky room." Cave Johnson Couts's eldest son spent a lot of time at the property, even spending nights there as a way to shield his horses from eager bandits. It was known that Couts Jr. had one of the greatest collections of horses. Felipe Subria also built a three-sided barn for his horses and raised cattle and sheep. In terms of residual paranormal events, there are cases of lingering aromas and smells from long ago. This is the case with the horses that lived on this property, as many guests have acknowledged odors associated with these animals throughout the rooms in the adobe.

About two years ago, as we were taking our tour group through the makeshift chapel, a female attendee announced that she noticed the strong permeating smell of hay, which seemed to dissipate just as fast as it came into being. About twelve months ago, while conducting the Spirits of the Adobe 9:30 p.m. tour, another guest encountered the pervasive phantom stench of horse manure in the exact space that was originally labeled the stinky room. There would be logical explanations to these ghostly aromas if living horses existed adjacent to the Rancho Buena Vista property; however, there are none close enough that they could cause these intermittent smells. The City of Vista administration building is across the street from the adobe to the south. Residential units are to the east, and other businesses and even a school lie toward the west. Wildwood Park is situated just north of the property. Thus, we have deemed these olfactory paranormal encounters to be residual supernatural events.

In addition to these spirited scents, both Ali and I have verified phantom sounds on the property associated with this ethereal horse. In 2016, about halfway during our private San Diego Paranormal Research Society investigation of the adobe, we heard the squealing sounds of a horse. The event was extremely brief, lasting only about a second. Additionally, the sounds were localized to where we were situated inside the adobe rooms. Since there aren't any living equine beings near the vicinity of the property, we knew that we were most likely dealing with yet another residual paranormal phenomenon. Just to be extra meticulous, we both went outside for a while to survey the animal sounds. All we heard were the normal sounds from typical wildlife that reside on or near the property.

We have also documented hearing the phantom sounds of a horse's gallop throughout the adobe. This has occurred more or less in the sala, as opposed to other rooms. It's not an extremely loud phenomenon; it's more on the faint side, but it's something that you can easily distinguish.

Known as the "stinky room," this is the original adobe space where Cave Couts Jr. kept his prized stallion away from horse bandits. *Author's collection.*

Various guests have reported these equine sounds, which seem to consist of about three or four gallops. Again, these noises point toward more of a residual phenomenon from the adobe's earlier days. Is Cave Couts Jr.'s prized stallion forever imprinted on the Rancho Buena Vista Adobe property? Since he was such a revered animal, it would make sense that he is.

As mentioned, Ali Schreiber is very knowledgeable about horses, as she used to own the beautiful animals during her younger years. Throughout our tenure as tour hosts at the adobe, Ali has proposed various questions about equine life to the spiritual residents. In addition to other profound spirit vocalizations regarding these animals, we received an emphatic "yes" to Ali's question, "Do you have a five gait?" Five-gaited horses are known for their ability to conduct five unique horse gaits, as opposed to the three gaits of walk, trot and gallop.

MOOCH, THE FELINE MASTER OF THE ADOBE

Frank Rojano has worked for the City of Vista for many years. As you know, he also provides security services for the Spirits of the Adobe tours. One night while we were at the adobe, he told us about a cat that once lived on the Rancho Buena Vista premises. According to Frank, this feline belonged to one of the last owners of the adobe prior to the City of Vista taking hold of the estate in 1989.

As part of our paranormal research at the property, we started to ask questions about this cat named Mooch. In March 2017, we initially asked if Mooch was present with us and our tour attendees while we were all standing in the master bedroom. I inquired, "Is Mooch the kitty here tonight?" A ghostly male vocalization occurred right after, saying "Mooch." Every single person developed goose bumps, as the response was so loud and clear. We didn't recognize the voice, so we are obviously unsure as to who answered our question.

It seems as though via our questioning we've been able to develop a rapport with this intelligent spirit cat. We do not feel that he is residual in origin, a psychic imprint in time, but rather possesses intelligence and a desire to interact with the living. Many of our tour guests have asked about Mooch, especially during a collective group spirit communication session. Intriguingly, it seems as though he can comprehend our queries, as people have documented possibly seeing a phantom cat just seconds after we ask about him. This has occurred several times on different evenings inside the sala or great room in particular. In December 2017, as we were escorting the tour group through the beautifully ornate archway leading into the adobe's courtyard, Ali announced that she saw a fast-moving, small white figure move in a left-to-right motion. This occurred in the space to the left of the dining room and kitchen. Ali further shared that the entity she saw was low to the ground and resembled a small animal. Could this have been Mooch?

During a collective group spirit communication session in the sala, one female tour guest announced that she felt a small animal brush up against one of her legs. She said it felt as though the fur from a small cat touched her leg. Just to be sure, we all made sure that a wild animal hadn't accidentally come through one of the adobe's open doors. Once we confirmed that wasn't the case, we were left with questions as to what this animal could be. Was this Mooch making his presence known? If so, perhaps, he felt comfortable around this particular guest.

Above: One of the bedrooms during the Weil period, circa 1957–73. Today, the room houses many different artifacts hailing from various areas in Europe. *Courtesy of Vista Historical Society.*

Left: Apparitional sightings have been seen in this doorway separating the bathroom from the gathering room. *Author's collection.*

There have been times when Ali and I, as well as visitors, have documented hearing the ghostly sounds of a cat's meow inside various adobe rooms. Just recently, while in the sala, a phantom cat vocalization was heard just moments after addressing Mooch. Additionally, a couple of meows were heard emanating from the children's room adjacent to the majordomo room. Ruling out that a living cat was wandering the outside and inside confines of the adobe, we were left with a strong possibility of paranormal interaction.

OTHER SIGNS OF PHANTOM ANIMALS

There are living wildlife species that visit the Rancho Buena Vista Adobe from time to time. These include the region's coyotes, squirrels and owls. There have been several occasions when adobe visitors and tour attendees witnessed white, misty and translucent apparitional sightings outside the glass door in the sala that looks out onto the courtyard. These phantom findings resemble the shape of a small animal as opposed to the lady in white, who's also spotted along the adobe's veranda. Now, these smaller specters could,

When you look at this photo, it is easy to see why so many people choose to get married at the Rancho Buena Vista Adobe. *Author's collection.*

in all actuality, be oddly shaped reflections or an actual sighting of wildlife inhabiting the area. However, one constant remains clear: all the sightings through this door have the same intriguing characteristics, that match those of ghostly apparitional sightings. They are translucent, abnormal forms that move at impossibly quick speeds—all hallmark signs of a supernatural sighting.

CHAPTER 8

DOES A SPIRITUAL PORTAL EXIST ON THIS LEGENDARY SITE?

Based on personal experiences and/or intriguing scientific evidence, the majority of spiritual experiences at the Rancho Buena Vista Adobe seem to revolve around those ethereal energies that have a historical connection to the property. In lieu of this, the San Diego Paranormal Research Society has endured other mysterious happenings that suggest the possibility of a portal on the premises, mainly due to spiritual experiences there with some of our departed loved ones. Thought to exist at many haunted locations around the globe, a portal is explained as being a connecting bridge or passageway between our mortal world and the afterlife. Its purpose is to permit an easy, lucid flow of communication between the living and departed. No one knows how a portal is formed, as the process is equally as uncanny as any type of paranormal phenomenon. To be fairly honest, its concept is most likely to remain elusive indefinitely.

The concept of a portal may cause some anxiety for some people who don't have an in-depth understanding of the paranormal realm. To some, a portal is thought to bring in negative and unwanted energy. While this may be true for some sites, please know that the general spiritual ambience at the Rancho Buena Vista Adobe is full of positivity. Just as a hearing aid may help someone to hear, a portal helps spiritual energies to manifest enough so they can commune with the living. Think of it like a bridge connecting two planes of existence. The multitude of profound and historically relevant spirit encounters at the Rancho Buena Vista Adobe suggests that something exists there that's innately aiding its ethereal residents to speak with the living.

A modern-day view of the adobe's front space and well. Imagine being one of the earlier residents and looking out onto the sprawling, vast hillsides during a typical Southern California sunset. *Author's collection.*

There are many articles that attempt to describe portals and energy vortices. *Supernatural* magazine's article "Spirit Portals and Energy Vortexes" includes the following definition: "In simple terms, a spirit portal is a doorway in the physical world that allows free access to and from the spirit world. The existence of a portal can rely on a vortex of energy to sustain it." Intriguingly, this piece also suggests that portals can be categorized according to their types of energy flows, such as upflow vortexes or positive portals. It goes on to stipulate, "This is where the energy is flowing upward out of the earth, these vortexes are generally revitalizing and feel positive." Whatever the case, there is indeed something beautifully spiritual about the Rancho Buena Vista. Ali and I are consistently filled with gratitude for being able to experience the site's mystical energy on a monthly basis.

In 2016, both Ali Schreiber and I experienced profound paranormal encounters with our dearly beloved family members while co-hosting one of our tours. My insightful experience occurred in the master bedroom while we were conducting a live audio session. We were in the middle of asking questions of Cave J. Couts, as he has communicated with us in this space before, when my maternal grandmother and grandfather came through. I didn't hear them in real time; it was only when I reviewed our audio a few days later that I heard their exact vocalization speak to me. My grandfather Andrew F. LoPinto, MD, came through first, saying, "Nicole, I love you," followed by my grandmother Helen LoPinto saying, "Fulvio, go home, dear." Needless to say, when I heard these familial echoes, my body burst out in goose bumps while a warming feeling infiltrated my soul.

Andrew F. LoPinto was a renowned physician and obstetrician who owned his own practice in San Diego for many years. Much of the city's Italian community saw my grandfather for medical purposes. Helen LoPinto was a homemaker who was happily married to Andrew for over fifty years. They lived on East Alder Drive in the Kensington area of San Diego.

Of course, there is no scientific proof that my grandparents actually communicated to me in spirit form. But here's the kicker: Fulvio, albeit an uncommon name, was my grandmother's nickname for her husband, Andrew F. Lopinto. No one outside of his wife or the immediate family knew about this cute little moniker. Furthermore, the two voices that resonated through our audio gadget matched my grandparents' mortal voices exactly. Thus, there isn't a doubt for one single second that my beloved relatives

The master bedroom, where we've communicated with the spirit of Cave Johnson Couts. *Author's collection.*

106

spoke to me on this mysterious evening at the Rancho Buena Vista Adobe. What was it that enabled them to come through so clearly?

This profound incident strongly supports the notion that ethereal energies communicate to one another beyond the mortal veil. My grandfather told me he loved me, and also his departed wife, Helen, spoke to him and told him, "Fulvio, go home, dear." What did she mean by that? Perhaps Andrew momentarily left the comfort of heaven's pastures to visit the mortal world as a way to communicate with me, his granddaughter. Then, by Helen speaking those words to him, it was her way of reminding him that he needed to come back to heaven's paradise after he was done talking to me. This was a beautiful moment in time, as I had the chance to hear my grandparents in spirit form. This blissful encounter further demonstrated that Andrew and Helen are still together and continuing their lives in spirit.

There have been other incidents with the ethereal world that further support the notion of an existing portal at this legendary Vista rancho. While in the majordomo room one night on our 9:30 p.m. tour, a very fascinating occurrence took place involving the RMS *Queen Mary*, a legendary British ship that's currently retired and moored in Long Beach, California. For the past fourteen years, I have conducted intense historical and paranormal research aboard various areas of the liner; thus, it's safe to say that many of the ship's ghosts and spirits know me. An avid enthusiast of the *Mary*, I have written three books about the vessel, including *The Haunted Queen of the Seas: The Living Legend of the RMS* Queen Mary; *Spirited* Queen Mary: *Her Haunted Legend*; and *RMS* Queen Mary: *Voices from Her Voyages*.

At the time of this encounter, we were communicating with a male ethereal entity that mentioned my name. This was an entity that we haven't heard before at the adobe. We were asking questions about his origins and whether he has a connection with Vista, the Rancho Buena Vista or other nearby adobes, such as the Rancho Guajome or the Rancho Vallecitos de San Marcos. We didn't receive any replies to suggest this, so I inquired, "I am just going to ask; is this someone from the *Queen Mary*? Can you please say yes or no? Did the person that just said my name, is this someone from the *Queen Mary*?" About three seconds later, a male specter answered by saying "ship." How did this particular spiritual energy know that the *Queen Mary* is a ship, as we never alluded to this or even offered a remote hint? It's these types of ghostly intelligent occurrences that further spark interest as to how and why ethereal beings can display intellect. Perhaps we will never know the reason why.

Both Ali and I have experienced our names being said through spirit communication gadgets at the Rancho Buena Vista. Perhaps the spiritual energies know us so well that they feel comfortable addressing us by our names. Or are they being assisted by some portal that helps ethereal beings better converse with the living? It's hard to say either way. In 2016, on one of our tours, a breathy female vocalization came through echoing "Nicole." It was so clear that we all emphatically heard and comprehended what was said. Moments after, I said, "I thought I just heard my name." The guests replied with, "Yes, you did; that was very clear." Ali then asked Ysidora Bandini de Couts if she said my name. We didn't get a reply after, but considering that we've come to somewhat recognize spirit vocal intonations at the rancho, we can conclude that the aforementioned voice that said "Nicole" sounded quite similar to the Couts family matriarch.

Later that night, while we were situated in the master bedroom, the name "Nicole" came through our communicative gadget once again. The vocalization sounded eerily familiar to the earlier one. Its female cadence was light and breathy. Right after it was said, Ali imparted, "It said it again." So I then asked, "Who is saying my name? It's perfectly okay, but can you let me know who you are? Can you tell me your first name?" A very faint, seemingly ethereal answer comes through, saying, "Ysidora."

We mortals had a very eerie but almost divine encounter during a 2015 Spirits of the Adobe tour. While we were situated in the majordomo room, we consistently heard ethereal female weeping emanating through our spirit communication device. Immediately, our attention turned to Ysidora Couts Gray, as historical records indicate that she was extremely saddened at her loss of the structure due to foreclosure many years ago. Did we hear her weeping in modern time? If so, this would indicate a residual phenomenon, an experience from long ago that pulsates in the present. Needless to say, we addressed Ysidora and asked her if there was anything that we could do. Seconds later, Ali's device stopped scanning on a very sacred yet emotional song. Of course, we can't definitely explain this particular experience, but there may be some sort of message in it.

Obviously, animals can communicate to the living in spirit form, perhaps even more so than we can once we cross those pearly gates. You recently read about a feline by the name of Mooch that inhabited the adobe during its later years, in addition to the disembodied sounds of phantom horses. Another eerie but beautiful encounter with our departed furry friends occurred in the sala. You see, I lost my extremely beloved cat, Max Montgomery Strickland, to cardiomyopathy in February 2016. Since his peaceful passing into the heavens, Max has made his spirit form known quite often and in many places where I have been present. As you have deduced, one of these sites included the Rancho Buena Vista Adobe.

Upon review of audio files from a late-night private paranormal investigation of the adobe, I heard a phantom feline meow that sounded strikingly similar to Max's vocalization. I compared this spirited meow to a video clip of Max when he was alive as a way to analyze. To no surprise, really, both excerpts matched entirely. Furthermore, I have heard Max's ethereal voice many times in my house, so I am quite accustomed to the vocalized sound. Perhaps Max has found a friend in Mooch and visits the hacienda during Spirits of the Adobe tours or private San Diego Paranormal Research Society projects.

Ali Schreiber also experienced a profound spiritual encounter with the spirit of her mother while in the adobe's sala grande. Ali's mother passed away from complications due to breast cancer in 2015. Her passing was abrupt for the family, who only learned of her diagnosis two short weeks before her passing. She had told her children, "Don't worry, I'm not going to die." She began therapy, but after about eight days, she suddenly became unable to communicate verbally, and less than four days later, she faded away. Ali, the eldest child, knew there was so much her mother wanted to say but didn't have the time. She knew her mother never expected to pass on so quickly and there was information her mother would have wanted her to know if she had realized what was about to happen. Ali always thought of her mother as brilliant—absolutely the smartest person she knew. Ali relied on her mother's knowledge and wisdom, so when she passed away, Ali felt suddenly a bit lost.

The memorial service was beautiful, but Ali felt uncomfortable with family and friends looking on with pity and making uncomfortable small talk, and although she made it through the memorial service, she simply could not handle dealing with the "after party." No, it wasn't a party, per se, but as is normal with her faith, the deceased's family gets together following the memorial service with food, conversation, etc. Luckily, that night, there was a Spirits of the Adobe tour at the Rancho Buena Vista Adobe. Many visitors feel that being at the adobe is very comforting and the spirits that dwell there are familiar and welcoming, so Ali chose to attend the event in lieu of the family gathering.

On this particular evening, there were about seven to eight guests investigating with Ali and me. During the Spirits of the Adobe tours, we would normally conduct a recorded questioning session in the sala. This night was no different, except this time, Ali agreed to use the dowsing rods. Dowsing rods (or divining rods) are a metaphysical tool commonly used by paranormal investigators to possibly communicate with spirits or those that have passed on. The dowsing rods used by the SDPRS team are two L-shaped rods made of copper, with a dowel around the handle portion of the rod, allowing it to move freely. When holding the dowel portion of the rods so they are at a ninety-degree angle, the investigators then ask if any spirits are present, and if so, if they can move the free-floating rods in a certain way to indicate a "yes" or "no" answer to questions.

During this session, the rods seemed to be impressively responding to the investigators' questions. They directed the spirit that seemed to be interacting with them to cross the rods indicating a "yes" answer to their questions and to move the rods farther apart to indicate a "no" answer. As they began asking more questions, the rods moved in a matter to indicate that the spirit that was with them that night was a female, but she did not have any history with the Rancho Buena Vista Adobe. So was the spirit there because of one of the investigators or guests? When they asked that question, the rods Ali was holding crossed indicating the affirmative. Well, Ali had felt the presence of her mother that evening, but being a private person, she did not share that feeling with the guests on the tour; as a matter of fact, up until that time, she had not even shared the fact that she had just lost and buried her mother.

The tours are about the adobe and the spirits that dwell there, so Ali and I feel it's always important to keep questioning and such focused on the rancho; we don't feel it's ever necessary to make any investigation about us personally. However, on this night, when the rods indicated that the female spirit was there that night because of someone in the room, Ali and I knew that it was more than likely Ali's recently departed mother. At that time, Ali decided to inform the group of her mother's passing, and she thought it was best to keep the integrity of the investigation focused on the adobe, so she put down the rods and ended the session.

That's when something happened. As Ali was feeling emotional but always staying a bit skeptical, she couldn't allow herself to be 100 percent sure the spirit of her mother was speaking to her. When everyone stood up and the tour continued into the next room, a guest approached Ali and asked her if the name "Twyla" meant anything to her. Ali was taken aback; the hair on her arms was standing straight up. She asked the woman if she knew her or her mother, and the woman said no and then began to explain that during the recorded questioning session, she kept getting the name Twyla over and over in her head and felt compelled to approach Ali with the name to see if it was significant to her. It definitely was! Ali knew that name, as Twyla was the name of her uncle's first wife and she was a very good friend of her mother's back when Ali was a young girl. Wow! That, right there, was all Ali needed to validate that it was her mother who was communicating with them that night. Being the brilliant woman she was, Ali's mom probably thought, "What is the one thing I could say to make my daughter realize that I'm here?" She knew that Twyla was a name that was just unique enough, yet also so relevant to their family history, that she could say it to prove her presence. And, thankfully, the guest that night was open enough to hear it and pass that on.

Maybe not all of the spirits at the Rancho Buena Vista Adobe lived or worked there. Perhaps the adobe is a portal. Maybe spirits are drawn to the adobe for some reason. The beautiful Rancho Buena Vista draws visitors every day—maybe even the visitors we can't see.

Perhaps a portal is the main reason why spiritual energies are able to communicate so effectively and strongly with the living at the Rancho Buena Vista Adobe. Whether they are intertwined with the rancho's

Another scenic shot of the courtyard facing north. *Author's collection.*

historical narrative or not, it seems that ethereal beings can easily manifest and successfully interact with the living, day or night. We have conducted paranormal research projects in a variety of locations, including private residences, businesses and other historical landmarks, and have never had such consistently profound, contextual and historically relevant spirit communication as we have endured at the Rancho Buena Vista Adobe. In regard to the spirit world, there is indeed something beautiful occurring at this renowned Vista site. This is one of the main reasons why we, the San Diego Paranormal Research Society members, are so protective of the property.

EPILOGUE

Southern California's rancho period has made an indelible mark on the historical tapestry of the Golden State. This remarkable era epitomized freedom and incoming fortune not only for California but also for the many individuals who sought to have a better life. Sadly, many of these region's landmarks have dwindled away to fragmented pieces, a silent reminder of days past with quiet landscapes imbued with pioneer aspirations, dust-filled residences and enveloped herds of cattle. However, the Rancho Buena Vista Adobe has followed an entirely different fate, as it continues to stand tall and proud in modern times by pleasurably imparting its stories, memories and legends to visitors from all walks of life.

In recent years, the studies of ghosts, spirits and paranormal phenomena have infiltrated our core of existence. Even though there has been an imbedded intrigue in this realm since the dawning of man, a heightened interest has skyrocketed among the human race in recent times. Of course, there are many plausible reasons why; perhaps the cosmic universe is the main foundation behind it. Maybe it's an example of destiny being sealed long before its inception; in other words, perhaps research into the supernatural is an inevitable process for those living in modern society.

It seems as though the universe has chosen the San Diego Paranormal Research Society to answer the clarion call of communicating with the adobe's ethereal residents, who, in spirit, help to piece together its storied past by communing with the living. It has been a sheer honor to study and examine the legendary site's chronicles of time by delving deeply into its historical narrative and spiritual happenings. Undeniably, this renowned Vista location has aptly demonstrated how olden times and supernatural phenomena can collectively unify to convey the overall tales and legends associated with a historic landmark.

Surely, paranormal research exists as a way to keep the anecdotes and legends of yesteryear alive in the present. History speaks through the annals of modern time; it never dies, as there is always a palpable reminder of those who walked the land before us. The same can be said for spiritual entities that once inhabited a mortal framework just as the living do today—even though their corporeal days have ended, their souls continue to eternally thrive in present times by breathing symbolic life into their past so it pulsates in the present.

Both Ali Schreiber and I are forever grateful for the spirits of the Rancho Buena Vista Adobe, for they have all taught us a little something special about ethereal life beyond the stars. We have spent seven-plus wonderful years building a solid rapport with this site's beloved incorporeal residents; our plethora of profound spirit communication with them genuinely denotes how human consciousness can possibly survive physical death. Multitudes of intelligent spirit communications have consistently occurred here; on many occasions, we have been rendered speechless as a result—in a positive way, of course.

When you visit Vista, California, make sure to go see the iconic Rancho Buena Vista Adobe, where vibrations from long ago echo in the present. Open up your ears and soul as you walk through the beautiful site; by doing so, you will better appreciate its innate communicative whispers from within its walls.

Rancho Buena Vista Adobe
Historical Timeline

The following timeline is courtesy of the *Rancho Buena Vista Adobe History* pamphlet written by the Friends of the Rancho Buena Vista Adobe.

1836: Felipe Subria, a neophyte Luiseño Indian from Mission San Luis Rey, started to stake his claim on mission territory adjacent to the Buena Vista Creek. The grant was controlled by the Mexican government; on this tract, Subria reared some cattle and tended to his crops.

1845: Subria had to apply through specific channels in order to acquire a grant of land from the Mexican government. On April 14, 1845, he commenced the grant process by proposing a letter to Mexican governor Pio Pico, who held authority over the mission land. Pico subsequently signed the letter and tentatively approved the grant on April 28, 1845. It was then sent to Los Angeles and approved by mission representatives. In order for the Mexican government to endorse the grant, Subria had to agree to uphold a right-of-way of any roads or highways that crossed the property, set out the area's boundaries and document the natural landmarks to each corner of the property.

1845–1851: Felipe Subria maintained his garden and livestock for the many ensuing years, as he was too elderly to have discord with the Californios. It is thought that he constructed a small adobe house and a three-sided barn on Buena Vista Creek. This structure no longer exists.

1851: Maria de la Gracia, Felipe's daughter, wed William B. Dunn, an American soldier. Dunn was a private with General Kearny's dragoons. Subria gave Dunn and Maria the title to his property for one dollar as a wedding gift. The two newlyweds promised to care for him and the rancho.

1852: For a sum of $3,000, Dunn handed over the site to Jesus Machado. Machado then began to construct a permanent building out of adobe bricks. The rooms were complete with a thatch roof and dirt floors, with culinary operations held outside. In modern times, these rooms are known as the "gathering room" and the "stinky room." Jesus also built the first irrigation system for the rancho by damming the creek, thus creating a reservoir. Additionally, he dug a well to provide water for the residence and the orchard trees. He commenced the process to secure the title to the site via a tedious registration process with the United States government. The legal fees were quite expensive, so Machado resorted to many mortgages on the entire property.

1854: The owner of the Vallecitos de San Marcos Rancho, Lorenzo Soto, purchased the Rancho Buena Vista. He moved into Machado's previously constructed rooms and added an additional section of spaces, which led from the west to the east. These newly built rooms did not connect to the existing edifice. Soto passed away, and his wife relocated to San Diego after remarrying. She then sold the property to Cave Johnson Couts.

1866: Cave Johnson Couts became the new owner of the Rancho Buena Vista Adobe. He made subsequent improvements to the existing structures and added many rooms at the end of one building, including two verandas. He, too, did not connect the edifices. This rancho became the Coutses' second residence, as they also resided at the Rancho Guajome.

1874: Cave Johnson Couts passed away. His widow, Ysidora Bandini de Couts, became the manager of the estate. Their eldest son, Cave Couts Jr., spent a lot of time at the Rancho Buena Vista. He often shared his story of the *Rojo Bandito* (red bandit) who visited the adobe during one of his overnight sojourns tending to his horses.

1876: Ysidora Bandini de Couts transferred the site to her daughter Maria Antonia Scott and her husband, San Diego–based attorney Chalmers Scott. Scott was the Couts family lawyer prior to marrying Maria. Cave Couts Sr.

wanted the couple to have the rancho. Chalmers traveled a lot due to the nature of his business. So the couple did not officially make the adobe their home until 1879. They added on the large room (sala or la sala), which then joined the rooms that had previously been constructed by Machado and Soto, therefore making the rancho an L-shape. Sadly, the Scotts were frequently away from the property and endured many land dispute battles with squatters.

1887: The completion of Santa Fe Railroad tracks occurred between Oceanside and Escondido. Both Chalmers and Cave Couts Jr. (Maria's brother) convinced Maria to give the railway land for the rails. In return, Scott insisted that Vista be the location for a station or stopping place. This would ultimately assist local farms in having improved access to markets.

1891: Maria Scott sold the deed of the rancho to her younger sister Ysidora Couts Gray, whose first marriage sadly ended in divorce. She wed a second time to Judge George Fuller, who worked in Los Angeles. Thus, the Fullers could not reside at the adobe full time. However, they spent a good amount of money maintaining the site. The majority of the land and crops were under the auspices of Couts Jr. He filed many mortgages to finance the harvesting of crops.

During the Fullers' tenure at the adobe, they added rooms facing north and parallel to the original edifice. Prior to construction, they demolished an old kitchen that stretched off the last bedroom. The breezeway joined an addition to the main building. This new board-and-batten space was arranged into a modernized kitchen with a dining space and pantry, thus making the hacienda U-shaped. No supplementary additions have ever become a portion of the historic structure. With its twelve rooms, the rancho measured 4,189 square feet.

1912: Mrs. Fuller approved a forty-foot-wide path through the property for a road to Bonsall. At the time, Vista was starting to become an overnight stop for travelers moving north to Riverside.

1918: Ysidora Fuller deeded a right-of-way for the gas and electric company to install utility poles across the rancho property, therefore bringing electricity to the community and property.

1919: Ysidora Fuller sold the rancho to Jack Knight and his wife, Helen Louise. George Fuller passed away in 1918; financial debts and hardships in maintaining the property became too much for Ysidora. Mrs. Knight was a Colorado Cripple Creek gold mine heiress. The Knights reinforced the walls and roof and revamped the kitchen design to make it more modern. They also enclosed a breezeway on the west end and renovated it into a sizeable bathroom. A brand-new entrance to the courtyard, which is utilized as the entrance today, was established on the east wall. The Knights also installed a steam pipe heating system, complete with radiators in each room. They also added a guesthouse on the east side parallel to the adobe with two pathways leading to the main structure. This new addition included a kitchen, three bedrooms and two and a half bathrooms and measured 1,880 square feet.

1923: The Knights hosted a dinner party on behalf of the Vista Chamber of Commerce. It was at this event that the couple offered the community the adjacent land of Wildwood Park, which was deeded in 1925. Wildwood Park is located to the north of the Rancho Buena Vista Adobe.

1927: The Knights filled out paperwork for a water right-of-way to be arranged.

1931: Harry and Margarita Fischer Pollard bought the Rancho Buena Vista Adobe. They were credited with upgrading the adobe's interior spaces, including the upgrading of bathroom fixtures and constructed closets. They imported exquisite tiles from Mexico and Italy. They also hung heavy wooden doors from Europe between interior quarters. The Pollards also installed a composition roof to replace shingles and employed a landscape architect to improve the gardens. The gardener installed the courtyard's focal water fountain and constructed walls and colonnades spanning the length of each building. A patio was also established adjacent to the guesthouse, as well as flagstone pathways. The Pollards also added a garage to store automobiles.

1951: The property was sold to Mr. and Mrs. Frederick Reid. Mr. Reid was a geologist and a partner of the Golden Nugget Casino in Las Vegas, Nevada. The rancho became a summer residence for the Reids as they did not live in the home full time. The walls of the adobe were painted white.

1957: Dr. Walter and Anastasia Weil became owners of the property. This couple repaired the roof and replaced all pipes with copper piping, as well as installed central heating. Once residing in the rancho full time, the Weils constructed the Vista Medical Center and Pharmacy for Weil to continue his practice. His hobbies included music and playing the violin. It comes as no surprise that he christened one of the bigger rooms the "music room." Periodically, the couple opened up their residence to tours, with other historic homes placed on this tour list, which became a yearly event.

1972: Mr. and Mrs. Rudd Schoeffel purchased the property. Without altering the structure, they did augment some of the areas around it. They replaced some of the flagstones with Mexican pavers on the verandas. The couple also moved the driveway off Escondido Avenue to Alta Vista Drive. Eighty thousand bricks from an old Alcohol Beverage Control building in Salt Lake City were purchased to create the new driveway. Only sixty thousand bricks were utilized, with the remaining ones sold as a way to finance the installation of bricks. They demolished the previous garage constructed by the Pollards and replaced it with a contemporary one. An additional guesthouse was constructed, which was finished in 1980. The following year, the Schoeffels built the professional buildings on previous orchard land.

1989: The City of Vista purchased the Rancho Buena Vista Adobe.

BIBLIOGRAPHY

Bingley, Craig Gilbert. "Rancho Buena Vista Adobe History." Master's thesis, 1993.

Brackett, R.W. *The History of San Diego County Ranchos*. San Diego, CA: Union Title Insurance and Trust Company, 1951.

Cavalier, Lois Vaughan. Images of America. *Vista*. Charleston, SC: Arcadia Publishing, 2008.

Christenson, Lynne Newell, PhD, and Ellen L. Sweet. Images of America. *Ranchos of San Diego County*. Charleston, SC: Arcadia Publishing, 2008.

Copley, James S. "Buena Vista Rancho." In *Historic Ranchos of San Diego*. San Diego, CA: Union-Tribune Publishing Co., 1969, 73–77.

Cowan, Robert G. "Ranchos." In *Ranchos of California: A List of Spanish Concessions 1775–1822 and Mexican Grants 1822–1846*. Fresno, CA: Academy Library Guild, 1956, 20.

Doyle, Harrison. "100 Years of Magic: Vista History." *Vista Chamber of Commerce 100 Years of Magic Business Directory and Centennial Magazine*. 1983, 10–19.

Doyle, Harrison, and Ruth Doyle. *A History of Vista*. San Francisco: Hillside Press, 1983.

Engstrand, Iris. "California Ranchos: Their Hispanic Heritage." *Southern California Quarterly* 67, no. 3 (1985): 281–90.

———. *San Diego, California's Cornerstone*. El Cajon, CA: Sunbelt Publications, Inc., 2005.

Garrison, Myrtle. *Romance and History of California Ranchos.* CA: Harr Wagner Publishing Company, 1935.

Gunn, Guard D. "Pio Pico: Last of the Mexican Governors." *Southern California Rancher* (January 1946): 12.

Hanson, John Wesley. *The American Italy: The Scenic Wonderland of Perfect Climate, Golden Sunshine, Ever-Blooming Flowers and Always-Ripening Fruits: Southern California.* Chicago: W.B. Conkey Company, 1896.

An Illustrated History of Southern California. Chicago: Lewis Publishing Company, 1890.

Magliari, Michael. "Free Soil, Unfree Labor: Cave Johnson Couts and the Binding of Indian Workers in California, 1850–1867." *Pacific Historical Review* 73, no. 3 (August 2004): 349–89. www.jstor.org/stable/3642129.

Moss, James E. "Pages from the Diary of Cave Johnson Couts." *Journal of San Diego History* 22, no. 2 (April 1976). www.sandiegohistory.org/journal/1976/april/couts.

Porter, R.K. "Trial of Col. Coutts for Murder: Sketch of the Murdered Man." *San Francisco Bulletin*, October 15, 1866.

Rush, Philip S. *Some Old Ranchos and Adobes.* San Diego, CA: Neyenesch Printers, Inc., 1965.

Schreiber, Ali. E-mail message to author, January 15, 2018.

Sherburne, Cook F. *The Population of the California Indians, 1769–1970.* Berkeley: University of California Press, 1976, 44, 60.

Strickland, Norma. E-mail message to author, December 20, 2017.

St. Romain, Theresa. *Margarita Fischer: A Biography of the Silent Film Star.* Jefferson, NC: McFarland and Company, Inc., 2008.

Tracy, Fred. E-mail message to author, January 30, 2018.

ABOUT THE AUTHOR

A natural history lover, Nicole Strickland is a native of San Diego, California. She obtained her bachelor of arts degree in media arts and a minor in journalism from the University of Arizona in 2001. Having a passion for education, she then achieved her master of science degree in educational counseling from National University in 2004. She is licensed to serve as a K–12 school counselor in California and has been an educator with San Diego City Schools for over ten years. Nicole also works as a freelance writer and blogger in her spare time. Throughout her life, Nicole has always enjoyed reading, writing and paranormal research. She is the founder, co-director and case manager for the San Diego Paranormal Research Society (SDPRS), a well-respected team that has conducted projects at private residences, businesses and historical landmarks throughout California and out of state. With a natural ability to collaborate with the San Diego community and beyond, Nicole and the team have given numerous presentations and lectures about paranormal research at libraries, conferences and via on-site classes on investigation strategies.

Strickland has also been featured on a myriad of media outlets, including print, radio, television and film. She is the co-host of the popular Spirits of the Adobe tours at the Rancho Buena Vista Adobe and has been researching the site for over seven years. She also lectures about various supernatural topics at conferences, events and local libraries.

Strickland is the author of *Field Guide to Southern California Hauntings*; *The Haunted Queen of the Seas: The Living Legend of the RMS* Queen Mary; *Spirited* Queen Mary: *Her Haunted Legend*; and *RMS* Queen Mary: *Voices from Her Voyages*. Published by Schiffer Publishing, *San Diego's Most Haunted: The Historical Legacy and Paranormal Marvels of America's Finest City* will debut in the spring/summer of 2018. All of Nicole's *Queen Mary* books sell extremely well aboard the RMS *Queen Mary* in Long Beach, California. Strickland is also a writer and correspondent for *Paranormal Underground Magazine* and *Let's Talk Magazine*. She is currently at work developing future books, articles and blogs related to history, paranormal research and other subjects.

Nicole has been conducting extensive historical and paranormal research aboard the RMS *Queen Mary* for over thirteen years. She fell in love with the ship the minute she stepped aboard in 2005 and makes monthly visits to the *Mary*. Known nationally and internationally for her knowledge of the *Queen Mary*, Strickland has presented about the vessel's unprecedented history and spiritual activity at numerous conferences, events and libraries, as well as via print, radio and television. Over the years, she has forged strong friendships with other *Queen Mary* lovers who also possess admirable knowledge about the liner's thirty-one-year reign on the high seas.

In her spare time, Nicole loves to travel. Her favorite cities include New York and Savannah, Georgia. She also enjoys cooking, exercising, watching classic movies and spending time with family, friends and her two cats, Aeries and Kayli. Nicole currently resides in San Diego, California.

You can learn more about the author via her website at www.authornicolestrickland.com and www.spiritedqueenmary.com. The San Diego Paranormal Research Society's site is www.sandiegoparanormalresearch.com.